AUDITION MONOLOGUES for YOUNG WOMEN

#2

More contemporary auditions for aspiring actresses

GERALD LEE RATLIFF

MERIWETHER PUBLISHING LTD.
Colorado Springs, Colorado

Meriwether Publishing Ltd., Publisher
PO Box 7710
Colorado Springs, CO 80933-7710

www.meriwether.com

Executive editor: Theodore O. Zapel
Assistant editor: Nicole Deemes
Cover design: Jan Melvin

Library of Congress Cataloging-in-Publication Data

Ratliff, Gerald Lee.
 Audition monologues for young women #2 : more contemporary auditions for aspiring actresses / by Gerald Lee Ratliff. -- First edition.
     pages cm
 ISBN 978-1-56608-193-1 (pbk.)
 1. Monologues. 2. Acting--Auditions. 3. Women--Drama. I. Title. II. Title: Audition monologues for young women number two.
 PN2080.R36815 2013
 812'.045089287--dc23

                            2013024557

1   2   3   13   14   15

CONTENTS

PROLOGUE 1

CHAPTER 1
AN AUDITION BLUEPRINT 3
Christine — *The Phantom of the Opera* (Gaston Leroux) 13
Eve — *Eve's Diary* (Mark Twain) 14
Elfie — *The Easiest Way* (Eugene Walter) 15
Heather — *God in Bed* (Glenn Alterman) 17
Jenni — *Six Foot Even* (Deron Sedy) 18
Deanna — *Pick Me* (Heidi Decker) 20
Hope — *Whole* (Scot Walker) 21
Mabel Lee — *Pretty for an Asian Girl* (Lucy Wang) 23
Kayla and Madison (Duologue) —
    My Conversation with Madison (Amanda Kozik) 25

CHAPTER 2
A TIME OF INNOCENCE 29
Phebe — *The Darker Face of the Earth* (Rita Dove) 30
Dotty — *Out of Sterno* (Deborah Zoe Laufer) 32
Marguerite — *Stamping, Shouting and Singing Home*
    (Lisa Evans) 33
Reggie Fluty — *The Laramie Project* (Moises Kaufman) 34
Narrator — *The Secret Life of Barbie and Mr. Potato Head*
    (Nin Andrews)...35
Amy — *Breathing Corpses* (Laura Wade) 36
Jessamym — *Some Unfinished Chaos* (Evan Guilford-Blake) 38
Marie — *A Bird of Prey* (Jim Grimsley).................................39
Myra Witzer — *Last Chance Romance* (Sam Bobrick) 40
Zahrah — *Slow Falling Bird* (Christine Evans).......................41
Cara — *Because of Beth* (Elana Gartner).................................42
Danny — *Blue* (Ursula Rani Sarma).......................................44
Teenage Girl — *Common Ground* (Brendon Votipka)...............46
Mrs. Harris — *The Columbine Project* (Paul Storiale) 47
Mother — *New Age* (Vivienne Laxdal) 48
Girl — *Baby in the Basement* (David-Matthew Barnes) 50

CHAPTER 3

A TIME OF REBELLION 52

Diana — *next to normal* (Tom Kitt and Brian Yorkey) 53
Polly X — *Trojan Barbie* (Christine Evans) 54
Twyla — *Underpants* (Wilma Marcus Chandler) 56
Sister — *Bunny's Last Night in Limbo* (Peter Petralia)................57
Laura — *The Arcata Promise* (David Mercer)............................58
Bonnie — *Third Person: Bonnie and Clyde Redux* (Peter Petralia)........60
Myrna — *The Mineola Twins* (Paula Vogel) 61
Ashleigh — *Thank You So Much for Stopping* (Halley Feiffer) 62
Kristen — *Bridewell* (Charles Evered)....................................64
Lisa — *A Preface to the Alien Garden* (Robert Alexander) 65
Cinderella's Sister — *Cinderella* (Chris Wind) 66
Julie — *My Battle with Bulimia* (Peter Langman) 68
Lily — *Glass Eels* (Nell Leyshon) 70
Peaches — *PEACHES* (Cristal Chanelle Truscott)....................72
Michelle — *Elephant* (Margie Stokley) 73
Samantha — *Samantha* (Sofia Dubrawsky)............................74
Woman — *Laughing Wild* (Christopher Durang)......................75

CHAPTER 4

A TIME OF INDEPENDENCE 78

Ma — *Soda Fountain* (Richard Lay) 79
Lexy — *Crispy Leaves* (Tara Meddaugh) 80
Olivia — *Ayravana Flies, or A Pretty Dish* (Sheila Callaghan) 81
Brett — *This Will Not Look Good on My Resume* (Jass Richards) 82
Miram — *Stupid* (Kevin Six) 85
Rivka — *In the Cards* (Caroline Russell-King) 86
Joanna — *God in Bed* (Glenn Alterman) 87
Sloane — *Something in the Air* (Richard Dresser) 89
Leena — *LUMP* (Leena Luther) 90
Cali — *Things of Dry Hours* (Naomi Wallace)........................92
Onatah — *On Sacred Ground* (Susan Rowan Masters) 93
Allegra — *Pretty Theft* (Adam Szymkowicz) 95
Intisar — *Veils* (Tom Coash)..96
Matilde — *The Clean House* (Sarah Ruhl)..............................98
Shawna — *Shawna* (Sofia Dubrawsky) 99
Rosalia — *Random Women* (Carolyn Carpenter) 100

CHAPTER 5
A TIME OF DOUBT 102
Veronica — *Miss Witherspoon* (Christopher Durang) 103
Evelyn — *Bums* (Robert Shaffron) 104
Millie — *Daughter* (Elana Gartner) 105
Grace — *Look What You Made Me Do* (Lynda Sturner) 107
Carol — *A Confluence of Dreaming* (Tammy Ryan) 109
Elizabeth — *Cold-Blooded Murderer* (Elisa Thompson) 110
Jessie — *In the Daylight* (Tony Glazer) 112
Amy — *All Aboard the Marriage Hearse* (Matt Morillo) 113
Nameless Woman — *When It's Over* (Christyna Belden) 114
Graciela — *Barrio Hollywood* (Elaine Romero) 115
Teddie — *Drawing Down Clio* (Doug Baldwin) 117
Actress — *Tirade* (Mary Louise Wilson) 118
Mother — *A Mother's Day Monologue* (Glenn Hascall) 119
Young Girl — *Tales from the Tunnel*
(Troy Diana and James Valletti) 121
Puerto Rican Woman — *Don't Breathe on the Job*
(Allen Davis III) 122
Gabby — *I Never Got to Say Good-Bye* (Lexanne Leonard) 124
Karen — *Six Views* (Lisa Kirazian) 126

CHAPTER 6
A TIME OF CYNICISM 128
Salima — *Ruined* (Lynn Nottage) 129
Roma — *Night Luster* (Laura Harrington) 130
Mitzi — *Baggage* (Sam Bobrick) 131
Carol — *The Pain and the Itch* (Bruce Norris) 132
Theresa — *Stain* (Tony Glazer) 133
Nameless Woman — *Funny* (Christyna Belden) 134
Michelle — *Sensitivity* (Lisa Soland) 135
Sabina — *Sleeping Dogs* (Philip Osment) 137
Critic's Wife — *New York Actor* (John Guare) 138
Gwen — *Let's Not Talk about Men* (Carla Cantrelle) 139
Gina — *Local Nobody* (Nicole Pandolfo) 140
Senta — *A Legacy for the Mad* (Don Nigro) 141
Lauren — *Beauty on the Vine* (Zak Berkman) 142
Petra — *Other People* (Christopher Shinn) 143

Young Girl — *Bad Boys* (Eve Ensler) 144
Teenage Girl — *Neverland* (Michael Edan) 146
Annmarie — *Chocolate Cake* (Mary Gallagher) 148
Kayla — *Enigma* (Carolyn Carpenter) 149
Rosie — *Better Places to Go* (David-Matthew Barnes) 151

CHAPTER 7
SCENE STUDY 153
Narrator, Girl, and Boy (Trialogue) —
Le Supermache (Ian August) 154
Karen and Bert (Duologue) —
Decisions, Decisions (Ken Friedman) 162
Dorothy and Auntie Em (Duologue) —
Yellow Brick Road (Paula Stone) 165
Juliet and Ophelia (Duologue) —
Anger Management (Lindsay Price) 167
Alice and Maureen (Duologue) —
Attic Letters (Jeanne Beckwith) 174
Lois and Fred (Duologue) —
Dinner for Two (Ken Friedman) 176

LEGAL ACKNOWLEDGMENTS 179

ABOUT THE EDITOR 189

PROLOGUE

"Life's Journey"

Some of us are born to travel life's roads — both high and low — on our own ... or alone. No one to share our highest moments or ease our lowest days. Alone — even in a crowd of friends — as strangers.

On guard against criticism and judgment at every turn. Pleaser by need — not design. Ever searching, never satisfied. Always needed, never enough. Life goes on ...

— Donna Rae Barker

CHAPTER ONE
AN AUDITION BLUEPRINT

"Acting is behaving truthfully under imaginary circumstances."
— Sanford Meisner, *On Acting*

There are a number of basic principles at work in this new collection of monologues and scenes for young women. Individual chapters are divided into "thematic" ages that introduce characters at a particular event or time in their lives. Each selection also includes a brief character analysis and an introduction that sets the scene and sketches the character portrait. The monologues and scenes selected for inclusion represent challenging character studies that you might expect to explore and perform in acting or literature classes, studio showcases, competitive auditions or forensic contests, and experimental workshops.

The fundamental principle that brings this sourcebook of monologues and scenes together is a challenge for you to visualize the dramatic and theatrical elements in each selection and to translate them into sensitive and complex performance portraits. The sourcebook suggests imaginative performance clues to pursue and encourages an individual style of character development that promotes fresh characterizations and original interpretations. Remember that even in a classroom setting or a more formal audition you are a creative artist, and the most essential ingredient in performance is an informed imagination.

The wider the range of life experiences and personal examples from which to draw, the more authentic and believable your character portrait is likely to be. The challenge, of course, is to cultivate a performance style that has a simplicity as well as a sincerity that is truly self–expressive. The strategies suggested in this introductory chapter lay a convenient foundation for defining the general characteristics of an imaginative audition and point out performance possibilities that may help you translate the basic theory of role-playing into actual practice.

The introductory chapter also provides a framework of basic theatre principles associated with the audition process and suggests an orderly system of preparation that should address any potential try-out scenario.

Basic Audition Principles

Audition characters do not leap full-blown from the printed page of a script. They emerge slowly in subtle and frequently disguised performance clues that point the way to creative role-playing opportunities for the actor. That is why it is crucial to search for an honest and truthful character portrait using your own personal experiences rather than looking "outside" yourself to fill in an author's tentative character sketch. Although monologues from scripts were not intended by the playwright to be performed independently as audition material, one of the reasons theatre directors request a monologue audition is that it gives them an initial hint of an actor's vocal and physical qualities. This first impression may include a wide range of objective and subjective responses.

- Does the actor have a sense of stage presence and exhibit an air of self-confidence?
- Does the actor voice character dialogue in standard stage speech or speak with a dialect or regionalism?
- Does the actor exhibit fluid movement and appear comfortable on-stage?
- Does the actor voice believable dialogue and create a three-dimensional character?
- Does the actor seem accessible and open to direction?

It is important to remember that the audition is an appetizer of your talent, not the full-course meal! The vocal and physical choices you make will suggest not only your potential acting skills, but also your stage personality. Don't be afraid to follow your basic instincts in an audition, but make performance choices that focus on vocal and physical strengths. Those choices should also reflect your age and emotional range as well. The challenge is to cultivate a three-dimensional audition performance that has simplicity as well as sincerity.

4

Choosing Audition Monologues

Preparing for an audition involves more than simply selecting a random monologue and memorizing the character's dialogue. When you are choosing a potential audition monologue, think carefully about what is appropriate for *you* as well as what you are auditioning *for*. It would serve no purpose to parade out your tried-and-true Charlie Brown monologue for a Shakespeare audition! The choice of monologue — either from this new collection or from another source — should also exhibit an emotional or intellectual range that is compatible with your life experiences.

Honest and simple are the basic ingredients for all auditions. Explore monologue characters that exhibit some variety in their emotions and overcome significant obstacles in their struggle. Look for monologue characters that suffer emotional anguish or experience a climactic resolution of conflict. Select monologue characters whose emotional depth or intellectual curiosity you can immediately define and understand. Final choices should be made with a burning desire that incites you to *want* to perform your character portrait at an audition. Remember, your objective is not only to demonstrate you might be right for a specific role but that you are also an actor with talent and imagination who might play a number of different roles.

It may be helpful to use active verbs that give vocal color and meaning to your final character's dialogue. Choosing active verbs to define a character's specific intention or motivation in the monologue should give vocal color and meaning to the dialogue and clearly underline a character's attitude or mood. Active verbs should encourage you to play monologue characters as *I* and to act in the *present tense* so actions and attitudes are fresh and spontaneous. Examples of active verbs to describe a character's intention or motivation might include to resist, to seduce, to ridicule, to expose, to obstruct, to humiliate, or to revenge.

A good performance idea is to try and identify a character's *moment before* the monologue excerpt. The moment before is that recent emotional, physical, or verbal incident in the script that propels the character — and you — into the monologue. Identifying the inciting incident may provide additional clues to the character's mental or emotional state that give your audition performance a more original flavor. It is also a good idea to compile a *memory book* of distinctive vocal and physical traits you have observed in others when sketching an audition character portrait. These random critical observations may help you portray more authentic character actions, postures, walks, or vocal patterns when you later assume the role of a fictitious monologue character.

Types of Audition

It is important to be aware of the types of audition and to be prepared for any requests made by the director. Some directors use a *cold reading*, where the actor is given a prepared or set speech of a character and asked to interpret the excerpt with little or no time for preparation. Cold readings give the director an initial impression of an actor's skills in interpretation and vocal or physical characterization.

Other directors prefer the more traditional *prepared reading*, where an actor memorizes and then performs a monologue of two or three minutes from a classical Greek period, Shakespeare, or contemporary script. The prepared reading audition may also include performing two brief, contrasting monologues from several historical periods. The prepared reading audition enables a director to more easily identify the level of potential talent available for possible callbacks and evaluate each actor's ability to distinguish character attitudes or moods. Still other directors like auditions that are *open* to all interested actors, or *closed* where only those who have been invited may attend.

A *general* audition, however, is the most common type and is used primarily to "screen" actors for more intensive group or partner work at a later callback. Each type of audition may also include *improvisation* — a brief sequence of impromptu exercises or theatre games — or a *directed reading*, where the director gives actors specific instructions in vocal interpretation or movement before asking them to perform a monologue or duo scene from the script being cast. Each of these types of audition is essential in the director's assessment of an actor's spontaneity, flexibility, and capability to follow direction — so be prepared for the unexpected, and may the creative force be with you!

Preview Principles

One of the first steps to take in previewing potential audition monologues is to read and analyze the complete script if it has been published. It is also important that you know and understand a character's changing attitude or mood in the complete storyline, rather than in an isolated monologue. When you read a script, pay special attention to what the character *says* and *does*. This background information should tell you "why" a character behaves or speaks in a certain manner. Unless you become familiar with the complex incidents that motivate a character's *action,* your audition performance may fall flat because it doesn't give additional meaning to the character's intention in the monologue.

In some ways, previewing potential audition monologues is similar to the journalist's use of the "Five Ws" to frame a news story. Like the inquiring journalist, you should ask and be able to answer the following questions about a monologue character: *Who* am I? *What* am I doing? *Where* am I doing this? *When* am I doing this? *Why* am I doing this? Once these preliminary questions have been answered, it will be easier to make more informed choices on the role that voice, body, and movement will play in an interpretation of the monologue character.

Audition Blueprint

There is a standard etiquette for auditions that every actor should be aware of as part of an orderly system of monologue preparation and rehearsal. Think of an audition as a job interview in which you are performing answers to some of the questions a director may not ask out loud. Should the director's first impression be "no" to any of the following questions, the actor may not be considered a serious candidate for a role in the production:

- Did the actor follow posted audition directions?
- Did the actor warm up vocally and physically?
- Was the actor an early or late arrival?
- Was the actor sufficiently prepared?
- Was the actor dressed appropriately?
- Was the actor courteous?
- Would I want to work with this actor?

To become more familiar with the special features associated with audition etiquette, please review the following practices. Remember that you have a limited amount of time to give distinction and individuality to your audition, so careful time management should be part of your audition blueprint. Although you will no doubt learn more about audition etiquette through personal experience, the basic principles that follow should guide you in pre-planning an audition routine that gives meaning and vitality to your performance.

Accents
Use character accents or dialects *only* if they can be voiced with accuracy and precision. Include a catalogue of standard audition accents — British, Cockney, German, Italian, Asian, Gypsy, New York/Brooklyn, Southern American, Spanish, and Midwestern — in your audition arsenal. It may be helpful to purchase accent tapes or learn the phonetic alphabet in order to cultivate meaningful dialect authenticity.

Auditors
Position yourself close to the auditors, but try to avoid actively engaging them as partners in your audition performance. You would not normally look an audience member directly in the eye while delivering lines of dialogue, so think of the auditors as invited guests at your one-person show and allow them to watch you rather than perform with you.

Off-stage Focus
The role of off-stage focus is an effective tool in placing characters or incidents "out" of the audition playing space in a straight or angled line slightly above the heads of the auditors. Off-stage focus also places the actor in a full-front position to direct subtle facial expressions toward the audience.

Stage Business
Stage business that advances the storyline or provides clues to character interpretation is limited in an audition. The most practical use of stage business to call attention to character behavior or habits involves small hand props: newspaper, fountain pen, handkerchief, cigarette lighter, mirror, or wallet, for example. Exhibiting subtle but

repetitive character mannerisms — cracking knuckles, yawning, stammering, or fidgeting, for example — to punctuate or underscore a character's point of view or state of mind may also be effective stage business.

Makeup

Light street makeup or a warm bronzer is appropriate for women. Remember that the role of makeup in an audition is to subtly accent facial expressions with a hint of color. Women sometimes wear their hair up or pulled to the side to highlight facial expressions. Do not rely on elaborate accessories like hair extensions, padding, masks, wigs, or prosthetic devices.

Movement

Movement in an audition is always relative to the playing space available and less likely to have a meaningful impact on a monologue. It may be helpful to consider physical business that underlines your character's point of view in the monologue and explore subtle variations in stance, posture, or gesture to suggest movement. The best approach is to maintain a healthy balance between movement that underlines a character's action and movement that accentuates the tempo or rhythm of the monologue.

Wardrobe

The audition wardrobe is simple and reflects the attitude or mood of the monologue character. The wardrobe should be carefully selected in terms of color, cut, or style with a focus on traditional designer principles of line, texture, and modest ornament. Warm and soft colors that complement the eyes and skin tone are particularly effective. Tight jeans, short skirts, flip flops, jogging suits, cut-offs, excessive jewelry, tank tops, and plunging necklines are inappropriate for an audition. You should also avoid platform shoes, sneakers, and high heels that tend to make stage movement awkward and unnatural. *Under no circumstances* should you wear a theatrical costume to an audition!

Callbacks

If you are called back for final casting consideration, it may be a good idea to wear the same wardrobe again to subtly remind the auditors of your initial audition. It is also important in callbacks to re-

read the entire script to review character attitudes and clarify character relationships. Do not anticipate the character role you may be asked to perform unless you have been informed in advance. You should, however, anticipate a cold reading, directed reading, improvisation, or series of theatre games as part of callbacks.

Props

Audition hand props should be limited to the small objects indicated in the monologue and easily handled without distraction — letter, pocket watch, glasses, cigarette lighter, diary, or handkerchief. Do not litter the audition space with an assortment of hand props that become part of your performance sometime later in the monologue. An audition is never about props or other theatrical accessories. An audition is always about how *you* fill an empty stage using only yourself as a prop.

Playing Space

Try to rehearse in the designated location before the audition date to explore the vocal and physical demands of the playing space. Pay special attention to stage or floor dimensions, entrance and exit doorways, seating arrangement, and acoustics. Being familiar with the playing space should help you combat the initial anxiety associated with auditioning in an unfamiliar environment. If you are unable to gain access to the scheduled playing space, rehearse in a number of different locations — classroom, dance studio, lounge, cafeteria — to anticipate later auditions that might not be held on a traditional stage.

Staging

Anticipate a limited number of audition set pieces: a single chair, stool, or small table. Do not consider monologues that require elaborate set decoration, ramps, special effects, or platforms. Stage *blocking* — directed movement in the playing space — should also be limited to focus attention on character intention or motivation. The most important element in staging is character *placement* in the playing space. Set up the space to face the audience, and be careful not to deliver your monologue in profile.

Placement

Recall the earlier discussion of off-stage focus and place imaginary characters in the audience or at a smart angle downstage center. Do not look down at the stage floor or off-stage while performing unless it is crucial to character development. Do not back up, turn around, move upstage, or wander aimlessly unless the script suggests such movement. Perform monologues in the center of the playing space, and move downstage right or downstage left as appropriate to underscore character action, attitude, or mood.

Warm Up

Don't forget to arrive at an audition at least thirty minutes in advance to warm up your voice and body. Regular vocal and physical relaxation exercises are essential to promote an expressive voice and flexible body. If you have discovered a number of your own relaxation exercises in the rehearsal period, use them as part of your audition warm-up routine.

Additional Dimensions

Begin to build a portfolio of monologues that represent different historical periods and styles for later auditions. The portfolio should include at least six to eight monologues with a performance time of two or three minutes each. The portfolio should represent a good mixture of comic and dramatic character portraits from classical Greek, period, Shakespeare, and contemporary scripts that have an obvious contrast in character attitude, mood, and point of view. Character portraits should also be appropriate for your age, vocal range, and physical type as well.

If your audition monologues have a recent history of stage production, make sure that you secure the *acting edition* of the script. The acting edition is a documented chronicle of the script's production history. It may include character interpretation clues, stage directions, or performance hints that surfaced in the rehearsal period or in the public production of the script. Acting editions are relatively inexpensive and may be purchased directly from script publishers like Samuel French, Inc., Dramatists Play Service, Playscripts, Inc., or the Theatre Communications Group.

Non-Dramatic Monologues

One of the challenging demands for an actor is an ongoing quest to discover imaginative and memorable audition monologues that have performance potential. Non-dramatic monologues are a popular adaptation for auditions because of the character *thread of action* that gives these genres their basic structure and unity. Non-dramatic monologues are usually excerpts from novels, essays, short stories, narrative poems, or diaries. They provide fresh and intriguing character portraits in comparison to some of the more familiar and shopworn monologues that strut the stage in today's auditions.

Adapting non-dramatic monologues for an audition involves ruthless editing to isolate memorable character actions and to build moment-to-moment anticipation and suspense that builds to a climax. It would be crucial in an audition adaptation to isolate the character's apparent conflict, improvise character actions, and paraphrase lines of narrative description. It would also be important to frame carefully crafted transitions that condense the dramatic action to meet audition time limits.

There is a caution, however, that auditors seeing and hearing unfamiliar non-dramatic literature performed as an audition monologue may be initially puzzled. It may be necessary in the introduction of the monologue to indicate its relevance to a more contemporary interpretation of a character's intention and motivation.

Although non-dramatic literature provides fresh and inventive character portraits, some auditions may explicitly state that monologues must come from published theatre scripts, so always check the audition call notice for specific requirements.

The following non-dramatic monologues have been adapted for classroom performance or competitive contests that call for a solo performance. As part of your initial performance preparation, focus on the tempo that underscores the attitude or mood of the character speaking. Assume a performance perspective that suggests only the present moment described in the adaptation. Allow the story being told to tell itself in the action being described. *Individuality* is still the benchmark in playing non-dramatic audition materials, so utilize the reservoir of your own life experiences — coupled, of course, with creative imagination — to forge a memorable and unique character portrait.

The Phantom of the Opera
by Gaston Leroux

Freely adapted from the historical novel — and allegedly based on a true story — this late 19th century Gothic mystery and romance is, of course, the text source for Andrew Lloyd Webber's long-running Broadway musical of the same name. Christine Daae, an aspiring and naïve singer at the Opera Garnier, is haunted by a "ghost," actually a horribly deformed musical genius named Erik, who nurtures her as his protégé. In this monologue, Christine describes her first harrowing encounter with the fiendish Phantom of the Opera to Raoul, her true love.

CHRISTINE: I had heard him for three months without seeing him. The first time I heard it I thought it was the voice of an angel. I never got the Angel of Music whom my poor father had promised to send me as soon as he was dead. I thought that it had finally come, and from that time onward the voice and I became great friends. It asked to give me lessons every day. The voice seemed to understand mine exactly, to know precisely where my father had left off teaching me. It was a curious thing, but, outside the dressing room, I sang with my ordinary, everyday voice and nobody noticed anything.

I did all that the voice asked. It said, "Wait and see! We shall astonish Paris!" It was then that I saw you for the first time one evening in the house. I was so glad that I never thought of trying to conceal my delight when I reached my dressing room.

Unfortunately, the voice was there before me and soon noticed that something had happened. I saw no reason for keeping our story secret or concealing the place which you filled in my heart. Then the voice was silent. I called to it, but it did not reply. The next day I went back to my dressing room and the voice was there. It spoke to me with great sadness and told me that if I must bestow my heart on earth, there was nothing for the voice to do but go back to heaven.

I feared that I might not hear it again so I swore that you were no more than a brother to me nor would be, and that my heart was incapable of earthly love. At last the voice said, "You can now,

13

Christine Daae, give to men a little of the music of heaven." I don't know how it was that Carlotta did not come to the theatre that night, nor why I was called to sing in her stead. But I sang with a rapture I had never known before. I felt for a moment as if my soul were leaving my body. Suddenly I heard a long, beautiful wail that I knew well. It was the plaint of Lazarus when, at the sound of the Redeemer's voice, he begins to open his eyes and see the light of day.

And then the voice began to sing, "Come! And believe in me! Whoso believes in me shall live! Walk! Whoso hath believed in me shall never die!" I cannot tell you the effect that the music had upon me. It seemed to command me to come to it.

Suddenly, I was outside my dressing room and in a dark passage and was frightened. It was quite dark, but for a faint red glimmer at a distant corner of the wall. I cried out. Then, a hand was laid on mine ... or rather a stone — cold, bony thing that seized my wrist. I cried out again. An arm grabbed me around the waist and dragged me toward the little red light. Then I saw that I was in the hands of a man wrapped in a large cloak and wearing a mask that hid his face. My limbs stiffened, my mouth opened to scream, but a hand closed it. A hand that I felt on my lips, on my skin ... a hand that smelt of death. Then ... I fainted away.

Eve's Diary
by Mark Twain

This adaptation from the author's separately published diaries of Adam and Eve reveals the humorous first impressions that Eve has when she encounters a bumbling Adam in the Garden of Eden. Eve is beguiling and whimsical as she navigates that ever-tricky boundary between initial rivalry and later enduring attraction. There is just enough giddy, fleeting fantasy here to suggest Adam and Eve may soon discover that they were "made for each other"!

EVE: I am almost a whole day old now. I arrived yesterday. It must be so, for if there was a day-before-yesterday, I was not there when it happened or I should remember it. Of course, it could be that it did happen and I was not noticing. It will be best to start right now, and not let the record get confused. For some instinct tells me that these details are going to be important to historians someday.

I followed the other Experiment around yesterday afternoon to see what it might be if I could. But I was not able to make it out. I think it is a man. I have never seen a man, but it looked like one. It has frowsy hair and blue eyes. It looks like a reptile. It has no hips; it tapers like a carrot; and when it stands it spreads itself apart like a derrick. Maybe it is architecture. I was afraid of it at first and started to run when it turned around. I thought it was going to chase me but by-and-by I found that it was only trying to get away. So after that I was not timid anymore, but tracked it along for several hours — about twenty yards behind — which made it nervous and unhappy. At last it was worried and climbed a tree. Resting, apparently. It looks to me like the creature is more interested in resting that anything else. A week later I tagged around after him and tried to get acquainted. I had to do all the talking because he was shy, but I didn't mind. When I found out that it could talk I felt a new interest in it. Now I love to talk, all day, and in my sleep too. If I had another one to talk to I could be twice as interesting, and would never stop. I tried to get him some of those apples but cannot learn to throw straight. During the last day or two I have taken all the work of naming things off his hands, and this has been a great relief to him, for he has no gift in that line. Whenever a new creature comes along, I name it before he has time to expose himself by an awkward silence. In this way I have saved him many embarrassments. Now I purposefully keep away from him in the hope that he will get lonely, but he has not yet. I shall talk with the snake. He is very kindly disposed …

The Easiest Way
by Eugene Walter

Based on a 19th century short story and melodrama, this adaptation features Elfie, an attractive but aging chorus girl with limited talent, who has taken "the easiest way" out and become a mistress to several wealthy men. Now chillingly cold and calculating with a rough edge, Elfie is slowly coming to terms with the aftershock of choices made and secrets left long buried. Here, she delivers a sober sermon to her friend

Laura about the strong bonds of sisterhood that exist between women like them … and the paths they have chosen to follow.

ELFIE: Was it my fault that time made me older and I took on a lot of flesh? Was it my fault that the work and the life took out the color, and left the makeup? Was it my fault that other pretty young girls came along, just as I'd come, and were chased after just as I was? Was it my fault the cabs weren't waiting anymore and people didn't talk about how pretty I was? And was it my fault when he finally had me alone, and just because no one else wanted me, he got tired and threw me out flat — cold flat? It almost broke my heart. Then I made up my mind to get even and get all I could out of the game.

The thing to do is to lie to all men — they all lie to you. Protect yourself. You seem to think that your happiness depends on this. Now do it. Listen. Don't you realize that you and me, and all the girls that are shoved into this life, are practically the common prey of any man who happens to come along? Don't you know that they've got about as much consideration for us as they have for any pet animal around the house, and the only way that we've got it on the animals is that we've got brains?

This is a game, Laura, not a sentiment. Do you suppose this Madison — now don't get angry — hasn't turned these tricks himself before he met you? And I'll gamble he's done it since. A man's natural trade is a heart-breaking business. Don't tell me about women breaking men's hearts. The only thing women can ever break is a man's bankroll.

Original Audition Monologues

Original audition monologues are a recent choice of actors today and may provide a more personal form of expression than traditional theatre scripts. Although original monologues share many of the same three-dimensional character life experiences, conflicts, or resolutions that you might expect to find in a more complete script, they are independent character sketches and not always from full-length published texts. Like non-dramatic monologues discussed earlier, there is always the caution that some auditions may explicitly state that monologues must come from published theatre scripts, so don't forget to check the audition call notice for specific requirements.

There are a number of original monologues and duo scenes identified in individual chapters of this collection. They are included to initially challenge you in classroom discussion and script interpretation or more formal audition settings as appropriate. The selected original monologues and duo scenes included in this collection should serve as excellent models as you begin to visualize a character's action, attitude, or intention in an abbreviated text. At this point, you should have a good sense of basic audition principles and standard etiquette practices. Here is an opportunity to translate some of those basic principles and practices into a more refined audition blueprint playing original monologue roles.

God in Bed
by Glenn Alterman

In this original monologue, Heather, a bubbly young woman in her early twenties, shares a startling and unsettling story with her best friend in an impromptu game of "Tell me a secret you've never told anyone else." Heather's gripping, heart-wrenching secret is a sobering account of a tragic car accident in which she is speeding home late at night, runs over an old man, and then leaves the scene of the mishap. Although Heather's deep-seated guilt and remorse is powerfully evident, she offers no clear verdict on the question of justice which must still be pursued ... regardless of the price to be paid.

HEATHER: It was an accident. The road was wet and I was tired. So maybe, I don't know, maybe I was driving too fast, can't remember. I just remember wanting to go home, get to bed. I made this turn at the top of Beekman Hill. And there was that curve, and the next thing I knew, there was this man, an old man, right in front of my car. I slammed on the brakes! But there was this sound, like a "thump." Next thing I knew, he was all over my windshield. Car swerved, round and round! I was trying to steer while looking right at his face, his blood dripping down my windshield! Spinning, swerving, until finally the car stopped. Just stopped! And it was quiet, just the rain. And I sat there, looking right at him, this old man on my windshield. His face this close to mine, his eyes were wide open. And all I could think was, "Oh God, Mister, please don't be dead."

I got out, went to the windshield, touched him, moved him. Nothing. There was no doubt, yeah, he was dead. Must have been about eighty, gray hair, raincoat, wedding ring ... wedding ring. He was married, probably had a family. I stood there in the rain saying, "I'm so sorry Mister, I didn't mean to kill ya." Then I looked around to see if anyone saw. No one. Then I ... I pushed him off the hood of my car, and he fell to the ground. Then with all my strength I rolled him over to the edge by the cliff. And with one last shove I pushed him over. He rolled down for what seemed like forever, through bushes and rocks. Waited until finally he stopped. Then looked around again, quickly got back in my car, drove home, and cried. My God I must have cried that whole night. They found his body about a month later. No one ever found who did it. It's remained my secret — until now. *(A beat. Then smiling.)*

So that's it, the one thing I've never told anyone. Some story, huh? You're the first one. Why are you looking at me like that? C'mon, now it's your turn, Tammy. Tell me your big secret, your one thing you never told anyone.

Six Foot Even
by Deron Sedy

In this dark and original monologue, Jenni, a psychologically troubled and emotionally damaged young woman, has been charged with multiple murders and is now videotaping her confession for the detective who has been interviewing her. This probing study of a serial murderess is played out against the backdrop of Jenni's memory of her father — and raises serious questions about the influence of that powerful figure on her later male relationships that inevitably led to murder. As Jenni peels away each layer of her psyche, another layer surfaces underneath, and yet another, until she reveals her true self: a deeply scarred young woman still trying to understand the lingering trauma and bitter legacy of childhood memories.

JENNI: Camera on? You ready? — OK. So, um, my name is Jenni. Let's see … Well, I enjoy sports … I'm a Virgo … I like men who are well dressed. That's extreeeemely important. If a guy's a slob, he doesn't have a chance, but I just melt for a suit and tie. And I like my men tall. Six feet tall, *exactly,* as a matter of fact. I guess I'm a little OCD. *(Strained, nervous laughter)* I have not had much luck with dating … Gosh, my first boyfriend, Trevor, was just the love of my life. He was six feet, which I like. *(Embarrassed smile of pleasure at the thought)* And he was a stockbroker, so that meant suits to work every day. And … this might sound weird, but he sorta smelled like my father. Is that weird? Is that weird that I like that? Anyway, things didn't work out … Obviously! No ring on this finger!

Ummmm … and then of course came Kevin and Manuel and Derek … They were practically exact repeats of my relationship with Trevor. That's when they label you an actual serial killer, right around your fourth or fifth victim. Oh … did I not mention how my relationships ended? Yeah, usually after a few months dating a guy, if I don't feel that spark, well, I have to end things. End … him. I probably should have put that out there at the beginning. Really, though, a girl has to look out for herself. There's nothing worse than you meet a great guy, and you think he's just perfect, but soon enough you discover that he's actually five foot eleven and seven-eighths, or some other inexcusable nonsense! Sorry …

But, oh, then there was Jean-Pierre. Mmmmm … Jean-Pierre. Exactly six feet, always in Armani. I so wanted things to work out between us. I tried to be good. I did. I'd make him breakfast, and I'd butcher the pets of any other girls who talked to him … My Jean-Pierre. Other than eventually ramming knitting needles into his larynx, I'd say I was a pretty good girlfriend. There was Steve, who worked at a Men's Wearhouse, so he'd get a discount on suits, and he was six even. But this one time he wore sweat pants, so I had to break things off. You know … things he needed to live. And then of course there was Danny. Oh, Danny, Danny, Danny. My Danny was so sweet. But he wasn't as into *us* as I was. Some guys don't appreciate a thirtieth or fortieth voicemail in an afternoon. Oh, why didn't you love me, Daddy? I mean … Danny. Anyway, that relationship didn't end well. Well, you know. You were there, with the handcuffs and all.

So ... There's your confession tape, detective. By the way ... nice suit. How tall are you?

Pick Me
by Heidi Decker

Deanna, a normally shy and introverted young woman, is convinced that being cast in a reality show will transform her life. In this fast-paced, explosively funny and devastatingly satiric tape that she is preparing for her audition, Deanna offers a series of character improvisations she believes will reveal her remarkably inventive theatricality. At times hip, outrageous, delirious, or demented, Deanna hits all the wrong notes and may have revealed more about her talent and herself than she realizes.

DEANNA: Hi! Hi! Hi! Um, OK. So ... so. OK. Hi. My name is Deanna, but all my friends call me Dazzle. I'm making this audition tape for you because I *know* I am exactly what you are looking for! Honest, I mean it. I have been watching reality shows my whole life! All of them. For real. I know all the stock characters and I've got them all down. Like ... OK, Tomboy Skater Girl! *(Grabs hat, puts it on backwards, slouches left, shoulders forward and arms crossed. Nods.)* S'up? *(Pause)*

Or ... or the quiet Goth girl who is secretly really artistic but totally misunderstood. *(Takes off hat, pushes hair into her face and quickly slips on black trench coat. She pulls out a drawing from the inside pocket and holds it up. Very dramatically)* This is a picture of *my soul.* *(Pause)*

Oh! I can also do the wild party girl who is secretly sad and lonely inside! *(Starts dancing and punching the air while making house music sounds. Shaking hair wildly)* Woo! Wooooo! *(Pause, then stage whispers sadly.)* When will I ever be loved?

Oh, ooooh, or I'd be really good at being the sweet and innocent girl from the country who is secretly evil. *(Wide-eyed)* Oh my, I've never seen such a big city before! I'm so glad I know someone smart and strong like you who can look out for me! *(Aside)* Can you *believe* this loser? Pathetic. Manipulating these idiots is gonna be too easy. Everything is going exactly as I planned. *(Evil laugh)* Ha, ha, ha, ha, ha!

(Back to herself) I know there's a time limit for this, but just so you know, I can keep going for days! You name it, I can be it. You need a tragic back story? Easy. You need me to have a crisis that changes the way I look at the world? I can rock that in my sleep. Need a foreign exchange student to spice things up? I can do accents. I can even be twins! *(Earnestly)* Any character you want. I'm your girl. I promise you, nobody wants this more than me. Nobody will work harder. I can make any of your realities real. All I have ever wanted is to be on one of your shows. Please. You have to cast me. You won't be sorry, and I really need this. Please. If you don't pick me, how am I ever going to know who I am?

Whole
by Scot Walker

Hope, an anguished and tormented young woman in her early twenties, is still shackled by a past childhood of heartache and sorrow that played out against a backdrop of stark emotional disappointment and despair. In this tender original monologue, she now reflects on the recent death of her mother and only then discovers the ties that truly bind them. Hope's reflections stress the special healing joy of self-forgiveness as well as her realization that there is also a place in the heart for mercy and repentance for a mother's undying devotion and love.

HOPE: I was a skinny girl in the summer between seventh and eighth grade — five two and barely eighty pounds — meat somewhere — but mostly ribs, lots of ribs and bones sticking out of everything. I remember getting a bathing suit that summer and wondering how I'd feel — listening to the other girls laughing at me, hearing them snicker, watching them point.

Mom said it was because I was always dancing, tip-toeing on my ballet toes across countless middle school stages. That, and the fact that

I was always running. Goodness, do I remember the running, down a thousand corridors to history class, racing past the eighth and ninth graders, wondering, worrying if I would be on time — and dreading the giggles I knew I heard behind my back, in front of my face, and even at my side.

That summer, that summer that I remember so extraordinarily well, my mother drove me to my junior high so she could have "a word" with the cafeteria staff. I needed a job, she said. I was thin but wiry — wiry, that's what she said even though I felt more like a puppet on a string — and I could help with the kitchen work, she said.

They couldn't pay me, they said. It was against the rules. They couldn't pay me … but they could give me a free lunch if that would be OK.

My mother sighed, her Irish sigh — and agreed. I'd wash dishes and get a lunch in return. But … how on earth I'd ever get to the cafeteria, gobble down my meal, eat, and not toss my cookies, I never knew.

I didn't sleep at all that summer — worrying about how fast I could run down that hall — running until I was able to beat the bell to the cafeteria, eat my lunch, and wash three hundred plates, three hundred knives, three hundred spoons, three hundred forks, three hundred trays. I cried a lot that summer too. Wondering why my mother was so mean, why she was so bent on humiliating me any more than I already was.

On the first day of school, my teacher told me to leave class ten minutes early so I could get to the cafeteria and eat before the other boys and girls. And it was as if God had stepped off a throne and spoken to me. I wouldn't have to run. I wouldn't have to choke down my lunch. I would be free. *(Pause)*

Last night, while going through my mother's papers, I found her diary — found out my dad had lost his job that year — that they had no money — they had no food. My Aunt Alice paid our rent, and my dad went through the missionary barrel at church. Without that dishwashing job I would have gone hungry. I might have … *(Pause)*

And now, my mother is dead, and I never knew. I never ever knew. *(Pause)*

I never had a moment to say, "Mom, thank you. Thank you so much for loving me."

Thank you for keeping me whole.

Pretty for an Asian Girl
by Lucy Wang

Mabel Lee, a deft and brightly intelligent teenager who exhibits unmistakable signs of puppy love, feels lucky that she gets paid to tutor the most popular, best-looking boy in her high school. She is startled to learn, however, that someone with whom she thought she shared a special bond could actually be a callous and rude bumpkin — until he pays her an outrageously insulting "compliment." Mable Lee's sweet dreams now collide with harsh reality as feelings surface and truths emerge. Although she is hardly the richer for the unfeeling behavior of her high school crush, she is certainly the wiser for the experience.

MABEL LEE: He said I was pretty for an Asian girl. And like a total idiot, I giggled and said thank you. I know, I'm pretty stupid when it comes to guys. Make that super stupid. I know how to get As, but that's about it. But hey, it was enough to get Trevor to ask me to be his personal tutor. Actually, his parents pay me. By the hour. Do you know how many girls would love to tutor Trevor? For free. I wanted to offer, but my mom and dad wouldn't let me do it for free. We need the money. We always need the money. Besides, they said it wouldn't be right — me wasting all that valuable time with a dumb boy. Dumb boy? Try the most wanted boy at Kucinich High. Seriously. He's so handsome. Popular. Athletic. It's really hard to concentrate when he flashes that smile. When his knees knock into yours. When he's staring back at you with those doey-eyes, full of mischief and wonder. Of course, it's not always dreamy. Sometimes you just want to scream or tear your hair out. How can he not know six times seven is forty-two? Sometimes you run out of explanations. Words. Logic. But that's Trevor's gift. He senses when you're lost or stuck, and breaks right through.

"You're so smart, Mabel Lee. I bet you're going to be a brain surgeon. Me, I'm more of a brain donor." I couldn't believe he called himself a brain donor! Today, he showed me a trick: how to get a shaker of salt to stand on one lonely salt crystal. It looked like it was going to fall, *(She tilts her body)* all tilted to one side, but it didn't. Aren't you impressed? I was. I'd never think of doing something like that. My parents are into order. *(She gestures tall, straight and narrow.)* Oh yeah, do your parents tell you you're pretty? Pretty? Did he say pretty or pity? My heart was racing so fast I lost count. Yeah, very pretty, Trevor pointed that sharp Number 2 pencil at me. My face felt really hot so I played with my hair, like those girls in the movies, and moved in closer because I thought he might want to kiss me, and I wanted to make it easier.

That's when he said, "Very pretty for an Asian girl." Thank you, thank you, but pretty for an Asian girl — what does *that* mean? Was this a joke? I pulled back. Aw, Mabel Lee, you and me, we're like apples and mandarin oranges. Apples and mandarin oranges, we're pieces of fruit? Exactly, we can't mix. What would our kids look like? Mongoloids? Mongoloids! Who said I wanted to have kids? I just wanted to share a kiss and a scoop of ice cream. I'm fourteen! *(Short beat)* Fourteen and unemployed. I quit. Actually I raised my rates, and Trevor's parents said they couldn't afford me. I thought my parents were going to kill me. But they didn't. They thought I was getting too boy-crazy, too distracted. They were right.

Original Duo Scenes

Original duo scenes are an excellent classroom introduction to the basic principles of scene study, initial character analysis, and a brief objective observation of life that explores authentic character relationships as if they had been "snapped" by a camera. The scenes, although unpublished, provide graphic representations of authentic flesh-and-blood characters that communicate directly and honestly with a minimum of exaggeration or artifice. These abbreviated scenes are a "picture" of reality, *not* reality itself, and are intended to provoke discussion, convey ideas, and enhance performance insights that may be useful in a more detailed analysis of the duo scenes that are included in Chapter 7.

Because original duo scenes are primarily concerned with the lives of ordinary people, classroom rehearsal and performance should focus on speaking and moving in a relaxed, distinctly personal and individual manner rather than exaggerated posing, elegant movement, or pretentious speech. The scenes also present imaginative opportunities to explore a character's *subtext* — the "hidden meaning" of a character's thought that lies just beneath the surface of the dialogue — and to identify the verbal and emotional tug of war between what a character *says* and what a character *means* in the spoken dialogue.

My Conversation with Madison
by Amanda Kozik

In this gripping but deeply moving original duo scene, two young women find themselves on an unexpected journey through painful memories of friendship, betrayal, and denial as they each take a backward glance at an incident that shattered their lives forever. The scene moves deftly in and out of the frame of reality with the characters sometimes speaking directly to the audience but never *looking directly at each other. Their interactions, however, deepen and then unravel a disquieting truth which will linger in the heart and mind for some time to come. What is left as the scene concludes is a disturbing awareness that the means have fallen far short of justifying the ends.*

(Standing Center Stage is MADISON, a nicely dressed young woman. KAYLA, another nicely dressed young woman, slowly walks toward her, but not quite looking her in the eye. Throughout the scene, KAYLA never looks directly at MADISON.)

KAYLA: *(Somberly)* It's weird meeting like this, the first time since we went to the hospital.

MADISON: So you heard I tried to kill myself?

KAYLA: *(Suddenly shouting) How could you do that? How could you be so selfish? How could you hurt us all so much? Didn't you think about anyone else Madison?*

MADISON: Whoa, whoa, calm down. *(Moves to touch KAYLA reassuringly, but KAYLA begins to pace back and forth.)*

KAYLA: *Selfish, that's what you are!*

MADISON: Selfish? You're calling me *selfish?* I was in pain, I was hurting — how was my need for the pain to end selfish?

KAYLA: I don't understand it. You didn't reach out to me — to your friends!

MADISON: I didn't mean to hurt you, to let everyone down. I felt you were better off without me. I felt worthless, and at the time it

25

seemed like ultimately I was helping all of you ...

KAYLA: This is so like you, always trying to do things by yourself, never asking for help. If you were depressed, you shouldn't have tried to handle it on your own. I didn't even know how bad you were feeling.

MADISON: I ... I thought no one noticed because no one really cared.

KAYLA: Why didn't you tell me you were depressed? *I'm your best friend!*

MADISON: I didn't want to burden you ... I felt so alone, I dunno — I just sort of forgot everyone else was there. I didn't think anyone really cared anymore ... and what could you guys do?

KAYLA: You should have told me, we could have talked! We could have found a way!

MADISON: It's not that easy ...

KAYLA: It may have hurt at first, but we could have worked through whatever was bothering you.

MADISON: Bothering ... that's putting it lightly.

KAYLA: Couldn't you see that you had everything to live for? You had your whole life ahead of you.

MADISON: Oh, sure ... a whole life of failure.

KAYLA: Is it because of your parents? Every time I'd come over to your house, I always worried about the way they talked to you.

MADISON: *(Looking at her feet)* Yeah ... they always wanted more in a daughter. They are so successful and I am average at best. It wasn't really their fault. I mean, I'm a failure. I ruin everything I touch. I totaled the car, then I started failing trigonometry — I mean, what the heck is tan? Why do you spell sign sin? I'm an epic failure.

KAYLA: I know they had high expectations, and I know that had to be hard. But didn't you see all the good things about yourself?

MADISON: Oh, like how I fell down the stairs and some guy caught it on camera? Yeah, a month of being a joke on the Internet was fun.

KAYLA: You shouldn't have let them get you down, Madison. You had friends, people who loved you.

MADISON: You were wonderful, but I was the problem, don't you see? I was flawed, and it hurt so damn much to be flawed. The pain was like a weight on my chest. It was hard to breathe. It started out as a dull ache, and then it just grew until all I could feel was the suffering in me like poison air in my lungs.

KAYLA: *(Pause)* You never saw yourself the way the rest of us did, Madison. Whenever I had a problem, you were always there. When Tiffany broke up with Brad, it was you who suggested a girl's night out. You always knew how to make us laugh — always. I guess ... I guess that's why I didn't realize you were hurting so bad. You had changed, but you were still joking ... still ... *(Pause)* ... oh my god ... You joked about killing yourself a week ago. How could I have been so stupid to not realize you were thinking about killing yourself?

MADISON: Kayla, it's not your fault! Don't even think that! I'm so sorry I didn't tell you I was thinking about suicide. *(Moment of silence)*

KAYLA: I'm sorry. I'm so sorry I didn't tell you how much I cared. I love you — we all love you.

MADISON: It's OK. *(Smiles sadly.)* From here on out I'll come to you, OK? You know, I felt like such a failure at the time. Dark thoughts filled my head. Now that I'm out of the hospital, I'm ready to get better. I've got my whole life ahead of me — a life worth living.

KAYLA: I guess this is good-bye. *(Wipes away a tear.)*

MADISON: Huh? What do you mean? *(KAYLA begins to walk away, turns and looks to the audience.)* What, are you not going to be my friend anymore because I tried to commit suicide?

KAYLA: I wish you knew how much we loved you ... It's kind of weird — I need you so much today. I think this would be easier if you were sitting in the back row, making your silly faces, making everyone feel better. *(KAYLA walks Stage Left and faces the audience.)* I'm sorry for running out of here earlier. I've not been in the best state of mind these last few days. The funny thing about having a friend commit suicide is how anger is a lot stronger than grief at first. You're angry at them for not turning to you instead of taking their life. You're angry at yourself for not doing more ... for letting it happen. But along with the anger there is this notable absence. I look out today and I see so many familiar faces — but there's one missing.

MADISON: Wait ... I don't understand. I'm standing right here. *(Looks down at her clothes.)* Why am I dressed up like this? I don't even remember the day I got out of the hospital ... I ... *(Pause)* Oh, no ...

KAYLA: I guess it's my turn to tell you about my friend Madison. Madison was what was right with every girl, what was right with every woman even. *(Pause)* She had the courage to express herself instead of following along blindly with the trends. She never thought of herself as smart because of her grades, but Madison had that quick wit and sense of humor that always brightened the room. She was silly, and fun, and kind. Her only flaw was that she couldn't see these things in herself. She always worried she wasn't thin enough or she wasn't popular enough. She saw only failures where those who knew her best saw triumph. Before I came in here, I said my real good-bye. I truly wish she had known how much she was loved.

MADISON: *(Faces the stage.)* Now I remember. *(Somberly)* I didn't *try* to commit suicide ... I committed suicide.

CHAPTER 2
A TIME OF INNOCENCE

"It is our fate to lose innocence ...
and once we have lost that it is futile to attempt a picnic in Eden."
— Elizabeth Bowen, *The Last September*

The characters featured in a time of innocence paint a rare portrait of complexity and discover wisdom in strange places. Their joys and sorrows capture those early years of youthful adventure, fearlessness, and idealism that will shape a later destiny. There is a sensitivity and rare sensibility in these sketches that is both searing and soaring, offering a fleeting glimpse of life that is at times funny, wise, and at the same time, very moving.

There is a uniform truth expressed by the characters in this chapter. Their experiences have taught them that human nature can be cruel and callous, with precious few moments of quiet escape from the reality of life. The authors reflect on the dizzying heights and emotional lows of heart-breaking romance, memories of things past, quirks of human nature, and the universal anguish and joy of living life to its fullest at a time of innocence — all without making judgments on their sentimental journey.

While plumbing the secret depths of young women's issues with passion and wisdom, the authors also unearth the heart-rending alienation, fear, rejection, and eventual self-discovery that inevitably lead to a young woman's lyrical self-confidence. For some, these monologues may be a rare psychological window-opening into a world where young women triumph over adversity and change their lives forever. For others, these intimate portraits may simply cast a chilling shadow of unflinching honesty or wicked humor, like stardust against the feminist horizon.

The Darker Face of the Earth
by Rita Dove

*In this contemporary version of the classical tragedy of Sophocles'
heroic figure Oedipus, who unknowingly slays his father and marries
his mother, former United States Poet Laureate Rita Dove unmasks the
lies and deception of an increasingly complex puzzle set on a plantation
in South Carolina in the 1840s. Phebe, born a slave on the plantation
but now a mature African American woman caught up in the
revolutionary ideas of a charismatic new slave named Augustus
Newcastle, brings her life into focus when she explains her mother's
death to him.*

PHEBE: Mama worked in the kitchen until
I was about five; that's when
fever broke out in the quarters.
She used to set table scraps out
for the field hands, and I
stuck wildflowers in the baskets
to pretty'em up. Mama said
you never know what a flower can mean
to somebody in misery.

That fever tore through the cabins like wildfire.
Massa Jennings said the field hands
spread contamination and forbid them
to come up to the house, but
Mama couldn't stand watching them
just wasting away — so she started
sneaking food to the quarters at night.

Then the fever caught her, too.
She couldn't hide it long.
And Massa Jennings found out.

(Gulps a deep breath for strength, reliving the scene.)

Mama started wailing right there at the stove.
Hadn't she been a good servant?
Who stayed up three nights straight
to keep Massa's baby girl among the living
when her own mother done left this world?
Who did he call when the fire
needed lighting? Who mended the pinafores
Miss Amalia was forever snagging on bushes?

Mama dropped to her knees
and stretched out her arms along the floor.
She didn't have nowhere to go;
She'd always been at the Big House.
"Where am I gonna lay
my poor sick head?" she asked.

He stood there, staring
like she was a rut in the road,
and he was trying to figure out
how to get 'round it.

Then he straightened his waistcoat
and said: "You have put me and my child
in the path of mortal danger,
and you dare to ask me what to do
with your nappy black head?"
He didn't even look at her —
just spoke off into the air
like she was already a ghost.

(Woodenly)

She died soon after.

Out of Sterno
by Deborah Zoe Laufer

Dotty, a cheerful but naïve young woman slow to come of age, lives a fairy tale Alice in Wonderland *life in Sterno — a small town located in the geographically undefined heartland of America — with her husband, Hamel. Although Hamel has forbidden her to leave their tiny apartment or to speak to anyone in their seven years of marriage, dutiful Dotty is content spending her days watching video re-enactments of the day they first met, working on kindergarten-style art projects, and breathlessly waiting for her lunk-headed, gas-pumping husband to come home for dinner. Here, an anxious Dotty takes a brief moment to extol Hamel's virtues — perhaps revealing much more doubt about her fairy tale life than even she realizes.*

DOTTY: First time I laid eyes on Hamel, I passed right out. He's got that kind of charisma. I was sixteen. He moved to our town from somewhere else. No one had ever done that before, so there was a lot of commotion. Every time I heard about him, I could feel my ears get hot. Then June third, two thirty p.m., I was at Joyner's store getting myself a chocolate Yoo-hoo, and in walks Hamel. He looks me over, does this *(Click, click)* with the side of his teeth and says, "Hey, kid." Well. When I came to, I see Hamel standing over me. He goes — *(She whistles.)* "What a nut!" And a week later we were married! Now we live in Sterno, which is a huge huge city, and Hamel works at the Mobil oil station, and we're so much in love! It's like a fairy tale, it really is. I don't exactly know anyone here, yet. Hamel doesn't much like for me to talk with other people. He's so crazy about me, he wants me all to himself! I love that. I bet it took a while for my mama to get used to never seeing or talking to me, but like she always said, "Make your man the center of your world, and you'll never get lost." I haven't actually ever even left this apartment! Not since we moved in seven years ago. *(Reacting to the audience)* No, no — that's A-OK with me. This is just about the greatest place on earth! All this and at six fifteen sharp, Hamel himself. *(Looks at a kitchen clock.)* Four minutes to Hamel time! So any of you ladies who are prone to fainting, get out your smelling salts!

Stamping, Shouting and Singing Home
by Lisa Evans

Marguerite, an intelligent, proud, and mature African American young woman trapped in a world of brutality and savagery reserved for Black Americans in the Deep South of the 1950s, decides to strike back against bigotry and injustice. In this gripping monologue, Marguerite describes for her mother and sister Lizzie a very real and dreadful episode of what happens when she tries to eat at a café reserved for "Whites Only" and the bittersweet reality of the world in which they live.

MARGUERITE: I didn't plan on staying out late, Mama. It was light when I went in. It was real crowded, but only a few folks sitting outside at them pretty tables on the sidewalk. So I went and sat there too. Folks were staring like I come from Mars or someplace. You think my skin green not brown. But I didn't take no notice. I sat at a table and waited for the waitress. Pretty soon she come out and took an order from the table next to mine. Then she goes back inside. Through the glass I could see white folks nudging and laughing at me, and the waitress talking to the manager. She come out with the order for the next table. This time I say, "Excuse me, Miss."

But she act like I wasn't there. No voice. No sound. But I heard my voice. And I heard it again when next she pass and I say, very polite, "I'd like a cup of coffee, please." I ask three more times but she carries on acting like I'm invisible. Then it come on to rain. But I sat on. I sat on while it got dark and they turned up the lights inside. And folks came and went and had coffee and cake and talked and laughed together. And I sat on. Pretending I didn't care. They weren't going to drive me away. Flood could have come and I'd have stayed, sitting in the dark, rain on the window panes, running down my back till I didn't rightly know if I was turned to stone. Some cars hooted as they drove off, laughing and yelling foul words. But I sat on. I had a right to be sitting there. I had a right to be served coffee just like they did. So I sat on. Then they closed up, put out the lights. I got up and come home.

The Laramie Project
by Moises Kaufman

In October of 1988, Matthew Shepard, a twenty-one-year-old student at the University of Wyoming, was brutally attacked, savagely beaten, and left to die tied to a cattle fence in the middle of the desolate prairie outside Laramie because of his sexual orientation. His bloody, bruised, and battered body was not discovered until the next day, and he died in an area hospital several days later. In a lyrically haunting interview with Reggie Fluty, a female police officer who first responded to a call for assistance when the young man was discovered, we catch a fleeting glimpse of the gruesome scene.

REGGIE FLUTY: When I got there, the first — at first the only thing I could see was partially somebody's feet and I got out of my vehicle and raced over — I seen what appeared to be a young man, thirteen, fourteen years old because he was so tiny laying on his back and he was tied to the bottom end of a pole.

I did the best I could. The gentleman that was laying on the ground, Matthew Shepard, he was covered in dry blood all over his head. There was dry blood underneath him and he was barely breathing ... he was doing the best he could. I was going to breathe for him and I couldn't get his mouth open — his mouth wouldn't open for me. He was covered in, like I said, partially dry blood and blood all over his head. The only place that he did not have any blood on him, on his face, was what appeared to be where he had been crying down his face.

His head was distorted. You know, it did not look normal — he looked as if he had a real harsh head wound. He was tied to the fence — his hands were thumbs out in what we call a cuffing position — the way we handcuff people. He was bound with a real thin white rope. It went around the bottom of the pole, about four inches up off the ground. His shoes were missing. He was tied extremely tight — so I used my boot knife and tried to slip it between the rope and his wrist — I had to be extremely careful not to harm Matthew any further. He was bound so tight — I finally got the knife through there — I'm sorry — we rolled him over to his left side — when we did that he quit breathing. Immediately, I put him back on his back — and that was just enough of an adjustment — it gave me enough room to cut him free there.

I seen the EMS unit trying to get to the location. Once the ambulance got there we put a neck collar on him, placed him on a back board and scooted him from underneath the fence — then Rob drove the ambulance to Ivanson Hospital's Emergency Room ... They showed me a picture ... days later I saw a picture of Matthew ... I would have never recognized him.

The Secret Life Of Barbie and Mr. Potato Head
by Nin Andrews

This charming original narrative is a romantic tell-all about love and passion that features the adorable doll-like Barbie and the affectionate Mr. Potato Head. Sharp and snappy, with bitingly funny innuendo, the monologue captures an incisive glimpse of two of the most celebrated figures in commercial industry and in the process dispenses a good deal of insider's dope on the dynamics of this romantic duo's relationship. It is a universal portrait of a young, spirited couple very much in love with the promise of many more happier but quieter years to come.

NARRATOR: It began the year Jane received her first Barbie, and Dick was given Mr. Potato Head for Christmas. Jane loved Barbie. She especially loved undressing Barbie. So did Mr. Potato Head. Soon Barbie and Mr. Potato Head were slipping off alone to dark corners. The first time it happened Jane's mother was fixing a salad for supper: cottage cheese nestled on a crisp bed of lettuce with canned pears on top. Barbie was nervously popping her head off and on. *"Jane,"* her mother called, *"Would you please set the table?"* That's when Jane told her mother that Barbie was engaged to marry Mr. Potato Head.

Of course even Jane knew Mr. Potato Head wasn't the perfect match for Barbie. She was afraid her Barbie might be jealous of all the other

Barbies in her neighborhood who had acquired handsome Kens for their husbands. But she soon realized her mother was right. Her mother always said looks aren't everything. Besides, Mr. Potato Head could make Barbie laugh. And he could do a lot more things with his detachable nose and pipe and ears when her mother wasn't looking. He, unlike Ken, was the kind of man who could change himself for a woman like Barbie. *"No problem,"* Mr. Potato Head would say whenever Barbie requested yet another body part.

Breathing Corpses
by Laura Wade

Winner of the 2005 London Critics' Circle Theatre Award, this macabre and madcap script takes its title from the classical Greek playwright Sophocles who said, "When a man has lost all happiness, he is not alive. Call him a breathing corpse." This contemporary interpretation features Amy, a naïve but clever nineteen-year-old chambermaid in an eerie, mid-price hotel, who has an uncanny knack for stumbling upon dead customers who have chosen to leave through express check-out. In this slightly farcical second run-in with a suicidal stiff, Amy wonders whether she will lose her job and shares her concerns while having an intimate conversation with an apparently attentive corpse.

AMY: *(Wipes her eyes and smiles weakly.)* I'm OK.
Just — you're dead and I'm going to get sacked I think, so —
Not very — not very good, is it? *(She laughs at herself.)*
Talking to you. *(She frowns, looking around the room.)*
That's new. *(She sighs and turns back to the corpse.)*
What's your name, Mr. Man? *(She turns back to the bed, pretending that the corpse spoke.)*

I'll go down and tell them in a minute. Probably think I'm joking this time. *(Beat)*
(Amy sees an envelope propped up on the dressing table.)
Oh, you did a letter. Nice. *(Amy picks the envelope up.)*
You know you look — I bet you were lovely. I bet you were really — really kind.

Not a person I'd ever really talk to but. But you look lovely.
Don't fancy you or anything, you're a bit old for me.
Probably got kids my age. Oh god have you got — *(Beat)*
(She looks at the envelope.)
Does it say in here? Who's Elaine? *(She turns the envelope over in her hand.)*
You didn't lick it. You know they'll take this. Evidence. She'll not get it for days.
She'll have a few days of not knowing why, while they're doing tests on it and stuff. If you've said why in here.
D'you mind if I — It's just you've not sealed it, so no one'd know, 'cept you and me and I won't tell anyone if you don't. *(AMY opens the letter and turns it over to see the name at the bottom.)*
Jim. Hi, Jim. *(She reads the letter.)*
Oh my god. A woman in a *box*. Like a cardboard box? God. Yeah, that's really hard. Hard enough finding you, can't imagine if I found one in a box.
Didn't you wonder about who was going to find you? *(AMY finishes the letter.)*
That's a really nice letter, Jim. I mean … For that kind of letter it's nice. Not too long, you don't blame anyone. Wouldn't seem fair, really, they never get a chance to say anything back. Good you haven't blamed anyone.
D'you mind if I open the window? It's just you smell a bit. No offense, but. It's just — You've had a stressful time, what with the — *(Gestures to the letter.)* and I think you've — on the sheets, so — *(She opens the window.)*
Cold out there.
Don't want to smell nasty when they come in, do you?

Some Unfinished Chaos
by Evan Guilford-Blake

Jessamym, from the "Princesses" monologues, is a talented and energetic young woman with dreams of being a writer and has persuaded a cynical, once-successful older author to help her with her writing. Their emerging mentor and father figure relationship is a touching portrait of two kindred spirits risking connection, rediscovering passion, and rekindling joy in both writing and in life. When her mentor is later seriously ill with cancer, he asks Jessamym to visit one last time. Here she recalls a childhood story that subtly masks her own unlikely journey these past carefree years and a renewed awareness of what is truly important in life.

JESSAMYM: See, when I was, I guess ten or eleven, I had a friend named Robin. She had the most beautiful hair, like Rapunzel. I had long hair too, but hers went on forever. They lived next door to us, her and her family. She was older than I was — fifteen or sixteen, I guess — but she was retarded. Not, you know, like she had Downs or anything like that. Just, she went to a special school, and she seemed like she was more like my age than hers. She used to come over to our house *all* the time, with her dolls, and we'd take turns brushing each other's hair, or we'd play — house, or doctor, or school, some little girls' game — or sometimes I'd read to her and she'd sit and smile … like she understood. Maybe she did, I don't know … I don't know.

Anyway. One day we were outside and I was brushing her hair and she asked me, she asked me if she could tell me a secret if I would promise to keep it. I was ten — of course I promised. And she looked all around and then she cupped her hands around my ear and she whispered, "I'm really a princess." "Really?" I said. "What kind of princess?" And she said, "I'm the Princess of the Rainbow. My daddy told me. Because of my hair. It came from the pot of gold. My daddy found it."

The Princess of the Rainbow. I've always wondered what happened to her. Whether she stayed a princess or … I don't know, I guess I wondered what — what it was like, to be her. To be — the way she was *and,* secretly, to be a princess ... and I wished, I wished *I* was a princess, that *my* father had told me *I* was one, that he'd — I don't know ... I love him but ... I don't know ... He used to call me "scarecrow." I guess that's why I wanted to learn to dance ... I was so clumsy ... I just wanted him to, I mean, I just wish he, *we'd,* I guess — loved each other, a little more. A little better.

A Bird of Prey
by Jim Grimsley

Marie, a sensitive young girl whose underlying insecurity and sorrow shines through, and her dysfunctional family have just moved from rural Louisiana to an urban environment in Southern California with calamitous consequences. But temptation and danger lurk around every street corner, and there is no comfort to be found from an increasingly abusive home life that mirrors the isolation and violence that Marie witnesses at school. In a moment alone on her way home from school, Marie confesses her need for the safety and protection of school and the emotional uncertainty of the family life to which she will reluctantly be returning.

MARIE: I'm going home. I'm walking behind Monty and Evan, and I'm being quiet so Evan won't punch me in the shoulder. I'm going home like I'm supposed to, but I don't want to go. All day in school it's been peaceful, with nobody bothering me, except Marie in my math class who hates that we have the same name. Except for her they leave me alone, and I like that. All day I sit there with my books and do what I'm supposed to do. Everything is calm all day. But school doesn't last long enough. I have to go home at the end of every day, and when the bell rings I get all hollow inside, and I pick up my books and go outside to wait for Monty and Evan. We walk home the long way, we go pretty slow, and we never talk unless we're arguing about something. We're all thinking the same thing, we're all wondering what it will be like when we get home, and I hate that feeling. I hate not knowing. I wish it would be peaceful. I think about it the whole way home, and sometimes it is. Sometimes Mama comes to walk us home instead of

Monty, and I can tell by the way she looks whether it's OK at home or not. If she's smiling and she's brushed her hair and if she looks me in the eye, then everything's all right. But if she's just standing there with her arms all wrapped around herself and her hair pulled back and she's looking at the ground, I know it's not OK. I know they're fighting again. I don't want to go home then, more than anything. But I don't have any choice. I wish school lasted longer. Sometimes I wish it lasted so long I would have to spend the night. I told that to my friend Candy. We have most of our classes together, and she likes me. I told her I wish I could stay in school all the time, but she didn't understand. She says I need a boyfriend, that's all I need. But I think about my dad and I don't know if I want one or not.

Last Chance Romance
by Sam Bobrick

Myra Witzer, a sharp-tongued and strong-willed woman determined to get married at any cost, casts a seductive spell on the timid and unassuming Leonard Shank. In this brief episode early in their courtship, Myra is visiting Leonard in the hospital after an accident that occurred while they were at the theatre. As Myra tries to make amends for the accident she may or may not have caused, we are left to wonder if Leonard's emerging romantic spirit will be strangled ... or will he recklessly embrace this last chance romance.

MYRA: Please, Leonard, I did not push you off the balcony. It was the end of Act One. I needed to go to the bathroom badly and you were blocking the way. I tried to scoot behind you and well, it didn't work out. I tell you, in a New York theatre if you don't get to the ladies room fast, you have to wait forever. They really have to do something about that situation. Maybe I'll mention that too in my letter to the *Times*. Anyway, Leonard, you didn't miss anything. The actors were so unnerved by your accident, their timing was off and the second act didn't seem to work as well as the first.

I knew if you lived you'd want to know how the play ended. I mean I wasn't worried that you wouldn't live but with the substandard conditions of the hospitals and the doctors all being unhappy about insurance payments, you never know what could happen. I've been telling people for years, if you don't have to go the hospital, don't go. Anyway, I'm happy to say you're looking much better than the Edelmans ... The couple you fell on. They're just beginning to feel sensations in their feet and the wife is almost able to speak whole sentences.

I beg you, Leonard, don't make me feel any worse than I do. By the way, that wasn't Al Pacino you saw. I checked it out. He was in France at the time attending a film festival. *(Holds out flower pot.)* Oh, this is for you. I didn't think you were into flowers so I got this instead. If you water it every day, in two months you'll have all the oregano you'll ever need.

Slow Falling Bird
by Christine Evans

Zahrah, a strong-willed and passionate Iraqi refugee, is being indefinitely detained at a detention center in the desert after her husband and children drowned en route to Australia. Although she and her newborn baby survived, Zahrah struggles to endure the harsh conditions of confinement and is plagued by recurring nightmares as she recalls the family's gruesome death. In this poignant character study, Zahrah tries to break through the web of grief and persuade her baby to feed as they both face a free, brave new world.

ZAHRAH: Why smile when time hangs like a dead bird in a tree? Good question, shark baby. *(Beat)* I'll tell you what. If you keep breathing, I will too. Just for now. Do we have a deal? Look at that white sun. Go on, look right at it. Not a scrap of yellow in it. Blinding. Go on, look at it.

Can't see it moving, can you? — I know you're looking — you're playing dead, but I can tell you're listening. Well, that sun is crawling down the sky's wall, like a fly. Yes, it is. And when it sinks, this red fleapit will vanish and so will the guards — until they turn on the floodlights and start the head count. But in that little breath between

41

day and night, well, this desert — could be the sea. You know there are fish bones in the desert, baby. From very long ago. And we can still see the stars, even older than the desert, tangled in the grid—wire like jewels.

Your daddy loved the stars. But by the time your brothers were born there were no more telescopes. No more science, except for the science of killing. So, we'd sit out on the balcony after dinner and he'd smoke, and look up at the stars and tell your brothers stories. How long it took the light to reach us. How we're just a fleck of dust in the eye of history.

Hear that, baby? That's the sound of wild dogs howling in the desert. I know it sounds scary but it's a good sign. Because ... because we're still out at sea. But when you hear that sound of dogs howling, it means we've nearly landed. And when you wash up on shore it will be quiet at last. So very quiet. You can hear your own heart beating and the tide going out, taking the boat and all its water — ghosts with it. Yes, you're stranded all alone — but the sand's still warm as blood, like a blanket. And by the time you notice how far out the water's gone, you won't be thinking about who's drowned. Because by then, the wild dogs of this land will be all around you. And that's the time to smile, my baby. Smile and show your teeth.

See, this is your country now.

Because of Beth
by Elana Gartner

This soul-searching original monologue explores a deeply felt moment of loss for a young woman who is both physically and emotionally devastated when she visits the grave of her recently deceased mother. Angry at her mother for dying and leaving a younger sister, Penny, in her care, Cara's burning emotions begin to explode as she shares the secrets that have surfaced after her mother's death. Here Cara confronts her mother's ghost with heartfelt honesty that makes their inevitable parting all the more poignant.

CARA: I'm really sorry, Mom. *(Long pause)* I know I should have been there. I had so many chances to say good-bye and you kept telling me ... say good-bye now, you never know ... and I didn't want to. Well, so, are you happy? You were right. You were right. *(Sighs.)* All that time and I never said good-bye to you. *(Finishes a cigarette and opens a beer. She sits down.)* And let's get something clear: I'm not saying good-bye to you now. That's not why I'm here. I came to talk to you. Just talk. You and me. *(Stands up and starts pacing.)* So let's talk ... *(Looks at grave. Short laugh)*

I always wanted you to listen to me ... Now that I have your attention, I don't know what to ... *(Long pause. CARA stares at the grave. Screams, frustrated.)* Aaaauuughhh! This sucks! I can't believe how much this sucks! You're not supposed to be gone yet, Mom! Penny? She's so whiny! It's like she has no other way to relate to me except to sob on me. And who do I have? No one! My friends aren't here. *(Pause)* None of these people today cared about you, Mom. *(Gets quiet.)* I did. I cared about you. *(Pause)* It's worse than when Dad left because at least then I had you. Now I don't have anyone. Oh, and what's with him showing up at the funeral? I mean, what is that, Mom? *(Angrily)* Since when does Dad even have a clue what is going on in our lives? Do you think maybe you could tell me that? It's sick, you know. It's like I only get to have one parent surfacing at a time. Well, luckily, he's gone again.

This is so unreal. You have to come home! You have to! *(Accusing)* You didn't even wait for me to show up so I could say good-bye to you! It wasn't my fault. I couldn't get here any faster! Couldn't you have waited just another fifteen minutes? And now Stanley wants to take Penny, the only family that I have left. It's not going to happen. Penny's my sister, not his daughter. Stanley wants me to go with him to the lawyers tomorrow. He said he thinks Dad's going to try to take Penny. *(Looks uncomfortable.)* Dad can't do that, can he? He hasn't been here in forever. He can't just come and take custody, right? *(Long pause as she thinks)* I'll have to be in the grave next to you for him to get custody, Mom! *(Quietly)* I'm the only one left who actually knows, who remembers everything about you ... I do. Even Penny doesn't.

I remember the night Dad left. No one else knows about that. *(Sits down next to the grave.)* Remember how you came into my room and you were crying … and you couldn't tell me what was wrong. But you just crawled into my bed and asked me to give you huggies to make Mommy better. And I did. I gave you huggies. But it didn't get better. And I started crying and we fell asleep crying. *(Long pause as she chokes back tears)* Mommy, I need huggies to make it better. I need huggies. Make it better. *(Starts sobbing and shaking. Rocks herself in her sobs.)*

Blue
by Ursula Rani Sarma

Daniella, a delicate and pensive tomboy with an unconquerable spirit, is an epileptic in her late teens who prefers to be called "Danny." Against the emotional landscape of taunting ridicule and a seemingly endless bout of personal insults, she is constantly bullied by the other girls in her class with a ruthlessness that is all the more bitter for its insensitivity. In this monologue, Danny gives voice to her affliction with a sensitivity that is riddled with heartbreaking insecurity as she searches for the words that best describe one of her fits after having been chased by some of the bullies.

DANNY: I lean against the wall for a while
and then I turn for home,
but they're still behind me,
they're throwing gravel at the back of my legs.
My head is still swimming.
Try to get away, have to get away.
(More laughter)
Debbie Wilson … I swear I …
(Breaks.)
I … please …
please …
I don't feel so good
(More laughter)
and my head is spinning and I'm screaming at them.
Something flips into place and I'm

44

tearing down towards the strand,
have to find the lads.
Joe Leary will sort you out you fat cow,
Or Des ...
Des ...

They're all on the strand,
the lads are playing football or skimming stones but
I'm looking for the lads,
can't see Des.
Mrs. Combers comes over and wants to know why won't
I play with the rest of them.
I try and explain,
there's a roaring in my ears and I can't hear myself talk.
*(Lighting change to isolate her, she physically reacts as if a needle
has been stuck between her eyes, in obvious pain for the rest of this
speech, it is slow and drugged.)*
Am I talking at all?
She's looming over me,
she's like a great beached whale, I think,
and then I tell her,
You're like a great beached whale, Mrs. Combers, did you
know that?
But the banging gets louder and louder,
and my leg starts to shake.
I'm looking at it,
(Falls to her knees, rocking forward and back.)
but I can't stop it,
and then the other one starts.
Mrs. Combers' face is getting redder and redder,
looks like it's going to explode.
I try to tell her but
*(Lights cut to a single strobe, she moves in the light for a moment,
rocking back onto her heels and then coming up to kneel facing the
audience, calmer now)*
it's like someone reaches in to my head and changes the frequency,
with a warm liquid hand, and all I can feel is a sweet heat spreading

45

up from my tummy and a smile to match on my face, and then everything is perfect, and it all goes dark.

Common Ground
by Brendon Votipka

Several teenagers sit at a table in a coffee shop and share their personal views on a number of topics while voicing sensitive and troubling confessions about themselves. The Teenage Girl, casting a vacant and unblinking gaze, struggles to find "common ground" with her friends. Instead, she paints a haunting self-portrait that is emotionally raw and painful that raises unanswered questions about ghosts of the past ... and perhaps the present. Her personal tug of war plays out chillingly with stark emotional contours that appear more like a voyage through the subconscious than a conversation with friends.

TEENAGE GIRL: I've been trying very hard to put into words the way I'm feeling right now. But I'm drawing a blank. I feel blank. "Blank" is almost something, but I fear it may be nothing. Nothing is an awful feeling. It's the absence of feeling. I don't feel nothing. Nothing is not what I feel. I feel something. Definitely something. I don't feel the absence of feeling, but I think I may feel the absence of color. Until I got out my art supplies from kindergarten, I couldn't decide what it was. Then, it hit me.

I feel like a white crayon. No, I don't. I am a white crayon. Exactly. I am totally a white crayon. I guess I always identified with the white crayon. The thing is, the white crayon just sits in the box. You following me? I mean, I know that all the colors sit in the same box. Back in grade school, when you bought your school supplies at the beginning of a school year, you could be sure that every color would be present. But while you can be sure they're all there, does it matter that every color is in the box? Does it matter if you have a white crayon? No.

The other colors get so much more action. Of course they get more action. Take a color like green. I wish I was green. Green is used in so many pictures, so often. How frequently does a kid use green? Pretty frequently. It gets a lot of action. Red is the same way. You use red for an apple, or a heart, or lips. Purple can be grapes, or flowers, or a sunset. Yellow, blue, brown, black, pink, any color, you name it! People use those colors all the time. A kid uses every crayon in the box.

Except white. No one ever picks up the white crayon. It sits in its box, completely sharpened and ready to go, but it's destined to remain in the stupid box. No one needs it. It has no use. I know, I know, "people use the white crayon sometimes." But rarely. Rarely. And besides, the white crayon is the crayon no one cares if they break. If they snap in two, no big deal. It's not like it's necessary for survival. No one needs a white crayon.

The Columbine Project
by Paul Storiale

Mrs. Harris — whose son Eric was one of the armed perpetrators of the Columbine High School bloody massacre in Littleton, Colorado that took thirteen innocent lives — speaks calmly as she gently folds the clothing her son was wearing when he killed himself. Although Mrs. Harris struggles with the painful memory and her own conscience, there is a profound sense of compassion, eloquence, and a painful self-scrutiny in the reminiscences as she agonizes over her own guilt with uncompromising candor. In the haunting face of rage and bewilderment at her own loss, she simply asks not to be judged guilty for her son's weakness.

MRS. HARRIS: I have no answers for what my son has done. I am outraged. Embarrassed. I have sorrows. The lawsuits filed against my husband and I speak for themselves. We must pay for the sins, religious, moral, and otherwise, with which my son has commanded unto this world. I extend my personal apologies to the communities in and around Littleton, Colorado, to the nation, and to the world, but no one listens.

As a mother, I have done all I could with the powers existent within me. With the advice of our family doctor, Eric was given a prescription for a drug called Luvox. I trusted this doctor. And, I trusted my son. A mother's intuition. I should have known. *But I did not know.* If I had known what my son had planned, this would never have happened. Eric has played video games since he was a young child. It's what kids do. It was not ignored or avoided. I understood the video games and music Eric purchased were not civilized, but (She thinks a moment) I suppose, I failed. I try not to blame myself, but I failed. Although my son was loved and attended to from the very beginning of his life. My husband and I loved our son and gave him as much attention as any parent. We share their hate for our son. It is unforgivable but not foreseeable. We share the sobbing questions, and we share in the grief, but let it be known that we are victims too. The witch hunt against us is ... Well, it's not fair even so. Their need to punish someone, somehow for this hideous attack is absolutely painstaking. The multimillion-dollar lawsuit that the Shoels family brought against us not only hurts but it angers me. Dylan and Eric are dead. They murdered these thirteen people and included themselves. We receive no empathy. We are badgered by blame for something no parent should ever endure. Yet I ask myself every day if there is anything I would change and my answer is no. I was tricked by my own flesh and blood like all of you. And I ask please, don't attempt to pledge me guilty.

The guilty are dead, and I was tricked too.

New Age
by Vivienne Laxdal

In this sentimental sketch, set in a maternity ward hospital room, the author probes the delicate relationship of a young Mother and her newborn child. Glancing warmly down at her baby's bassinette while he quietly sleeps, Mother shares her hopes and fears for what the future may bring her little angel. Her indomitable spirit and conviction only serves to strengthen the special bond and spirit a mother's love provides at a time like this. The dialogue is cleverly constructed — replete with sharp and amusing wit — and the child, as well as we, will be the wiser for Mother sharing her fears, hopes, and dreams with us.

MOTHER: *(Quietly)* Baby? Baby, are you sleeping? I've got some things to tell you, baby. Before you wake. Before I forget. Before you're too old to understand. I know you. You've just been born, but I've known you my whole life. And you know me, too.

You know me from the inside. You know my heart. I gave you my heart. Right at the beginning I gave you my heart. You know my breath. I gave you my air. I gave you my food. I gave you my water. I gave you my mind. It's OK though, you know? You shouldn't feel bad about that. No, not at all.

I'm going to know. I'm going to know what you're feeling. I'm going to know what you're thinking. I'm going to know what you're doing. Like nobody else in the whole wide world. I'm going to have eyes in the back of my head. That's what you're going to give me. And I'm going to be so proud of you. Every single thing that you do. Even when you fill your pants, I'm going to be the proudest person in the world. My baby. He did this. That's what you're going to give me.

And when you learn, I'm going to learn. I'm going to learn that a kitten feels soft. I'm going to learn that the sky changes color. That the rug is warm, and the floor cold. That the water is wet, that bubbles burst, that shoes untie. That's what you're going to give me. And when you hurt, I'm going to hurt. I'm going to hurt so bad. I'll take it all away from you. I'll take away your stomach cramps. I'll take away your baby teeth. I'll take away your diaper rash. That's what you're going to give me.

And when you are scared, I'll be scared. I'll be frightened of the fire engines. I'll be frightened of the barking dogs, the windy tree, the planes in the sky, of being alone. That's what you're going to give to me. And, when you are happy, we're going to hold hands. We're going to fly right up to the sky. We're going to giggle and laugh and cry and play and yell and shout and dance and sing. That's what you're going to give me. A few hours ago, I thought I was going to die, baby. I thought I was going to die. The pain would wash over me and drag me down to places I've never been before. I thought it would never stop. That I'd never come back. And I wouldn't be able to see your face. I wouldn't be able to hear you cry. I wouldn't be able to feel your small hand grasping my little finger. And then, I knew. That no matter how hard, no matter how long, no matter how painful, that you had to be here. That it had to be you and me. From now on. So this is it, baby. I had to tell you. Before I forgot. I knew you would understand. I am your mother. You are my child. Happy birthday, baby!

Baby in the Basement
by David-Matthew Barnes

A distraught and troubled teenage runaway stumbles into the dark basement of an abandoned warehouse in this complex monologue and inadvertently interrupts the suicide of a young man who is also hiding in the building. The Girl is sensitive and thoughtful as she and the young man initially share stories of the exasperating trials of growing up. Here, the Girl glows ever more brightly as she talks about an imagined "dream house" that can be built for both of them and change their lives forever. As she speaks, the boy slowly dies from a self-induced pill overdose and the Girl's dream house is forever shuttered in darkness.

GIRL: It's yellow, with shutters and trim around the windows. And there's flowers. Yellow roses and white carnations and even some daffodils. It's a beautiful house. It's not too fancy. It's simple. Like us. There's a basketball hoop in the driveway. And a dog. He's a golden retriever, and he's always happy to see us. And a porch — a real big porch with a wooden swing on it. A place where we can sit and watch the world walk by. *(The boy is lying down. She goes and sits next to him. She picks up the bottle of pills and holds them in her hand.)* At night, we can sit on the porch and look up at the stars and make a ton of crazy wishes on them. And our friends will come over and we'll feed them a ton of food and we'll play some cool music and we can dance. Someone will say something funny and you and I will look at each other and speak silently and we'll talk about things later. And in the summer, we'll save up our money and we'll go to Paris and we'll say a prayer for Shelley and we'll say her name, almost like she would be there with us. We'll take pictures and we will send postcards. Postcards to our families. Maybe they will miss us while we're away on our vacation. *(She looks to the boy and realizes that he is dead. She opens the pill bottle.)*

They won't miss me. They won't even realize I'm gone. My father will give his sermon. My mother will ignore me. My sister will damage her baby. Leave her in a basement. Just like this one. I would never do that to my baby. I would keep her warm and safe. I haven't even picked out a name for her yet. What do you think I should name my baby? I've only got five months to decide on a good one. Five months to get my life together. *(She takes a pill, swallows.)* What do you think of Tanya? Do you like that name? *(She takes another pill, swallows.)* I always liked the name Courtney. It's a pretty name. *(She takes a third pill, swallows.)* No. I will definitely name my baby Shelley. She was a good friend to me. *(She lies down next to the boy, pulls his arm around her so that he is holding her.)* I guess we got a plan, after all. *(Beat)* You're a sweet guy. You've got a cute smile. *(Beat)* I can't wait to see Paris with you.

CHAPTER 3
A TIME OF REBELLION

"Every act of rebellion expresses a nostalgia and an
appeal to the essence of being ... "
— Albert Camus, *The Rebel*

In a time of rebellion, the authors mix humor with occasional themes of alienation and self-doubt as their characters engage in a never-ending struggle to find a few moments of happiness or independence. Although rebellion may have taken up residence in their lives and cast a shadow of sadness or utter hopelessness on their views of the world, there is also a faint glimmer of hope that each character will eventually reconcile the past and bravely face a more rewarding future.

The characters fight, make up, spin dreams, deflate them, and then start all over again as they try to genuinely connect with other human beings for the first and, perhaps, last time. These are powerful portraits written with candor and compassion that address provocative ideas of frustrated characters struggling to live a meaningful life while coping with inner doubt, family strife, hormonal hysteria, or depression.

There is a startling resonance here that reaches beyond the narratives and touches so many nerves connected to alienation, betrayal, guilt, and self-image. These complex and almost hypnotic characters may not be the ones we are accustomed to seeing in our daily lives — or even imagining in our most disturbing dreams — but they are truly unforgettable. You may even come to learn more about yourself through listening to the stories, sorrows, and struggles of these others in their time of rebellion.

next to normal
by Tom Kitt and Brian Yorkey

This Pulitzer Prize rock musical paints a harrowing but lyrical portrait of smoldering anguish, drug abuse, and suicide that cripples a suburban family. Diana, a manic-depressive mother suffering with worsening bipolar disorder, struggles to escape the denial and pain that the battery of pharmaceutical and medical treatments have inflicted on her and those she loves. In these song lyrics, a fragile and gently tender Diana offers an uncompromising glimpse of a woman dangerously on the edge ... but still clinging to fading hope.

DIANA: Do you wake up in the morning
And need help to lift your head?
Do you read obituaries
And feel jealous of the dead?
It's like living on a cliffside
Not knowing when you'll dive ...
Do you know
Do you know what it's like to die alive?

When a world that once had color
Fades to white and gray and black ...
When tomorrow terrifies you
But you'll die if you look back.

You don't know.
I know you don't know.
You say that you're hurting —
It sure doesn't show.
You don't know ...
It lays me so low
When you say let go
And I say
You don't know.

The sensation that you're screaming
But you never make a sound.
Or the feeling that you're falling
But you never hit the ground —
It just keeps on rushing at you
Day by day by day by day ...
You don't know
You don't know what it's like to live that way.

Like a refugee, a fugitive
Forever on the run ...
If it gets me, it will kill me —
But I don't know what I've done.

Trojan Barbie
by Christine Evans

This modern retelling of Euripides' The Trojan Women, a bleak and agonizing portrait of war's brutality, features free-spirited Polly X as classical Hecuba's daughter Polyxena, sacrificed by the invading Greeks to Achilles to appease his ghost and bring a fair wind after the sack of Troy. Here, Polyxena is portrayed as a fretful, rebellious teenager confined in a women's prisoner-of-war camp after the invasion. Struggling to make sense of the fragments left of her beloved city and her own life, the modern Polly X explores the horror of war and the pain suffered by innocent victims.

POLLY X: Everything stinks here. I hate it. It stinks because we have to use gas for cleaning. Even the hospitals. For cleaning floors, toilets, wounds, everything. You can't get soap anymore. And since the fence, you can't even go out. There's nothing to do. It's foul. The whole country is like a poisoned stinky gas station just waiting for someone to throw a match. I am soooo over it.

Oh, I want to smell desert rain again. It hasn't rained for three years. It's probably because we're cursed.

Anyway. Before the fence, Mama took me to the museum so I would see our "Cultural Heritage." But it was all looted, except for the Contemporary Art. So — we had to look at *that* instead. The program said that "Transcendent Ideas of Beauty" are no longer what art is about. But actually, I just think we can't afford it. Like I said, it's hard to get stuff. So most of it was really ugly, and all made of broken things. Or things that really aren't supposed to be art. Like bottles and rags and old shoes and stuff just stuck together.

The most disgusting sculpture of all was called *Trojan Rat*. It had yellow eyes, and it was crouching in a pool of dark stuff that looked like oil, or blood, or something yucky. And it was hollow, you could see inside it because it was just made out of wire and plastic bags. Inside its belly it had a little white dining table, all tiny and perfect like real art. There was a family sitting 'round it, eating dinner.

But their house was bleeding and it was inside a rat.

Which had mean glittery eyes made of those yellow beer bottle tops that the soldiers leave lying around.

It made me feel sick but excited too.

I didn't like it but I did. I didn't but I did.

Mama hated it. She said it was "decadent and defeatist."

I said, "Well Hecuba, we are defeated."

She didn't say anything to that.

And then I decided: I *like* Modern Sculpture.

On the way home, I started thinking about things I could make out of my own broken stuff. Mostly what I've got is these —

(Showing Barbie dolls)

Most of them are a bit messed up, or they're covered in scribble and stuff.

Which is OK for Modern Sculpture. I'm going to get a big piece of pink cardboard. Helen says if you're nice to the soldiers, they'll get you stuff. And then I'm going to get all my dolls and nail them on to it. In the shape of a big heart. So when it's finished, it will be this huge heart, made of smashed up dolls. It will be sort of flat but sort of three-dimensional. It will be very, very scary. I'm going to hang it out the front of the women's tents.

And I'm calling it *Trojan Barbie*. And when it's done, me and Cassandra will rain down revenge on our enemies! We will smash them like dolls! Death to the invaders!

Underpants
by Wilma Marcus Chandler

Twyla, a mature, well-dressed woman with a sophisticated air of self-confidence and barely visible behind the many shopping bags she carries, hurriedly enters the lingerie section of a department store and pauses momentarily to catch her breath. She has been bargain hunting all afternoon, and her brief monologue is an engaging narrative in which Twyla recalls disturbing childhood memories of shopping for school clothes with her mother ... and might shed some light on her fascination with underpants!

TWYLA: I love to shop, I *know* everyone doesn't, but *I* do. I can just get lost in all the choices and then when I finally decide — I decide! It's like a good workout, you know? My husband hates it, but I don't think it's the actual shopping, but the *choosing* that wears him out. Doubt. Doubt. *(Laughs.)* It's a sad thing to see people fall by the wayside from self-doubt! Go for the burn, I say! *(Beat)*

It wasn't always fun, though. I've had to really work at it. My most vivid memory as a child is of shopping with my mother for school clothes every fall. I must have been about eleven or twelve ... very self-conscious, wanting to look just right all the time. My friend Myra Hirsch had a dress for every day of the school year ... I'm not joking ... her closets were amazing! Anyway, I mostly wore my cousin Edith's hand-me-downs, but that was OK because she had lovely taste in clothes and fairly free rein in choosing what she would buy each year ... except for that Kelly green camel's hair coat which I had to wear for *five winters* until my piano teacher finally said something to my parents about how my wrists were sticking out and getting very chilled and later in life that might cause arthritis ... *(Beat)*

Anyway, my mother would take me to "The City" to shop. We'd go on the train and would plan to shop all day looking for sales, having lunch. In theory it was always a spectacular event ... but this one time stands out because it was sort of a turning point for me. *(Beat)*

The first store we go to is having all these post-summer sales and my mother finds a two-piece gray and fuschia checkered seersucker suit

... sport top and dirndl skirt — hideous! She asks me if I like it. I believe it is an innocent question and I say *no!* but she looks at the price tag and says, "Let's hold on to it for a while" and she starts carrying it around the store while I look at Ship n' Shore blouses and Lanz dresses. Finally, after a few minutes she announces that the gray is my new school outfit. Her voice was very calm, as I recall, "Either this or nothing." Slap. Slap. I could see my whole year stretched out before me. I literally had *no* new clothes. I began to calculate. Is it better to get something new and hate it or wear all of last year's stuff? *(Beat)*

I would have behaved differently now. Now I don't care what anyone thinks. I took the outfit just to have something new, and I wore it and lived in shame all that fall ... every other Monday, and I always felt disgusting. No one ever said anything against it, but I felt such shame, both for the way I looked in it and for giving in to her.

Bunny's Last Night in Limbo
by Peter Petralia

Set in an eccentric household of whirling dysfunction, this original monologue has a touch of theatre of the absurd that distorts and exaggerates all the traditional icons of family values: a beauty-obsessed Mother, a drunken, media-crazed Father, and a lonely, embittered Sister. In this household, sarcastic put-downs and inventive oaths fly like knives, wounding all with tart personal insults. Here, Sister has reluctantly finished her household chores and begun playing with modeling poses and dance routines while drawing on her lips with lipstick as she shares her views on what it costs to be pretty and popular.

SISTER: I love l-i-p-s-t-i-c-k! All kinds. I've got ten shades of red and five browns. "I have a color to match my every mood." I got that from a Revlon commercial. Do you know the one I mean? It's with Lynda Carter. You know, "Wonder Woman"? She's in the swimming pool? Never mind. I can't imagine the world without lipstick ... it'd be pretty boring. I'd lose my favorite snack treat.

(She puts lipstick on and then bites a chunk of it. Then she puts it in her pocket as she chews the bite she took.)

L-i-p-s-t-i-c-k is the world's most overlooked source for nutrition. It's packed full of healthy stuff like vitamins and oils. It goes on smooth and digests right away. Mmmmm. Mary Margaret says l-i-p-s-t-i-c-k is made out of bat poop, but I don't believe her. She doesn't know anything about beauty anyway. Her mom won't even let her wear l-i-p-s-t-i-c-k. My mother thinks beauty is very important. That's why she is so pretty. She lets me wear makeup because she wants me to be pretty too. I'm glad because being pretty is fun ... and important.

I'm good at it, aren't I? I get all the boys to look at me. "My lipstick makes me look ... kissable." That's Maybelline. The boys in Mrs. Harper's class can't stop staring when I come in. I don't blame them. The other day on the playground I kissed a boy. He wasn't that good at it. I had to hold him down. He was chicken. He said he never kissed a girl before, so I asked if he had ever kissed a boy, and then he bit my lip. I got really mad, so I told everyone that he liked boys. He's dumb anyway. Everyone made fun of him. He's a weirdo.

(She takes out the lipstick again to take another bite. But it's empty — no more lipstick in the tube! She sticks her tongue into the tube, trying to lick out every last bit.)

Hmmpf! I'm gonna have to get some more. I think I want "Tragic Diva" this time, from Urban Decay. It tastes better than Maybelline. I think it's because it costs more. They put special things in it that make it good — and it stays on longer. I hope it's not bat poop. That Mary Margaret is crazy. They wouldn't put bat poop in there.

The Arcata Promise
by David Mercer

Laura, a fiery and fiercely independent young woman with a rebellious spirit, was only sixteen when her parents left her at school in England. Shortly thereafter, she met John, an actor in his early thirties, and — against her parents' wishes — moved to London to live with him. Now, four years later, Laura grapples with the harsh reality that her turbulent relationship with John is disintegrating as a result of his excessive drinking and obnoxious self-centered attitude. Alternating between sharp accusations and piercing insults, Laura now paints a sobering portrait of why she believes the couple are not *perfectly suited to each other.*

LAURA: I came to live with you because I loved you. I stayed with you because I loved you. *(Pause)* I endured you because I couldn't imagine life without you. *(Pause)* I feel battered. Ignored. Belittled. *(Pause)* I didn't care for you because you're a famous actor. You remember talking about that party where we met? Well, when you came over and talked to me, I thought I'd never seen a man so haunted. So defensive and uptight. *(Pause)* I never thought you'd find me attractive. I never thought you'd see me again. *(Pause)* When you asked me to, I said yes for you. Not because I was impressed, or flattered, or anything like that. I almost didn't dare to think you'd have any serious interest in me. *(Pause)* But you did. *(Pause)* Girls at school used to laugh at me because I said I wouldn't go to bed until it was somebody I loved. Very old-fashioned, or whatever. At my school you were considered freaky if you were still a virgin after sixteen. *(Pause)*

And because of you — I was glad. I was happy I'd never been with anyone else. *(Pause)* I've been happy with you — but sad as well. Too humiliated. *(Pause)* Too hurt. *(Pause)* I never thought it mattered at all, your being so much older. Now I can see it does. Not the years. Not the difference in experience. *(Pause)* It's that you'll go on being exactly the same. *(Her voice rising)* And I'm changing ... *(Standing)* I've loved you. I believe you love me. But you've lived and behaved exactly as you wanted — with me as some kind of appendage. *(Pause)* Where have I been? Who did anybody ever think I was? Some of your friends still can't even remember my surname! Others pity me. I can count on one hand the number of times I've ever been asked a question about myself. I imagine people find me dull and boring. You drink. You talk. You dominate.

I'm the one who drives you home. You rant. You rave. You're the evening's entertainment. I'm the one you turn on when we get home. I should think I'm despised. Not because anyone's taken the trouble to find out what I'm like. No. But because I must seem like your bloody shadow. *(Pause)*

⏎ Person: Bonnie and Clyde Redux
by Peter Petralia

In this original monologue about the dissolution of a love affair between two of history's most notorious lovers — Bonnie and Clyde — we catch an intimate glimpse of the electric attraction of their tempestuous love affair and doomed romance. Bonnie, a young woman who thrives on romantic tales of misadventure and struggles to break free of her suffocating small-town environment, stands at the kitchen sink making lemonade while talking to herself and an imagined Clyde who is not present. Bonnie's tone is warm and tender, but there is an undercurrent of haunting despair that foreshadows the couple's perilous relationship ... and eventual death.

BONNIE: Clyde, I used to want children. I imagined myself with little ones tugging on my apron strings, my handsome husband out in the fields working, and something good baking in the oven. I don't know what happened, but I cannot even imagine that anymore. Some people think we are cold-blooded killers, but we know that isn't true. Killing lacks passion; it's easy and mechanical, which is why love is for me. I love you, Clyde Chestnut Barrow. I do. We are just lovers trying to make a life for ourselves outside of a system designed for keeping us low. I am so tired of being pushed down. Tired of an empty pot on the stove. Clyde, I used to think I'd grow old in Texas, on a rocking chair watching the grandkids play. I don't know how I ever wanted that. I don't want to grow old, Clyde. I just want you to touch your hand to my face, to feel how soft it is. To kiss me. I'll never have any wrinkles. I'll never be anything but perfect for you, Clyde. And when we kiss, it will always be the first time. We'll die young, live fast, barely old enough to know any better. We won't have little ones running around our feet, but we will have each other. A few years living with you is better than a whole life of working the land, watching the injustice of life crash down around me. We'll live life like firecrackers, my sugar, and when our fuse burns out, we'll be together.

The Mineola Twins
by Paula Vogel

This satiric parable by Pulitzer Prize playwright Paula Vogel neatly captures the cultural and social undertones of today's political climate. Myrna — the "good" twin — and Myra — the "evil" twin — may share the twin bond but spend most of the time defining themselves in opposition to each other, both in their lives and in their beliefs. Here, a now mature Myrna parodies the biblical story of the "Prodigal Son" to persuade her own son, Kenny, to commit a white collar crime that will finally rid them of the evil twin, Myra.

MYRNA: You know the story of the Prodigal Son? This man had two sons, right, and one worked hard in the fields from dawn to dusk. He never gave his parents cause to worry. The other son never saved one thin dime, and he drank whatever money he filched from the family business. The Prodigal Son got into trouble with the law. He had to hide in this foreign land far across the borders, and a price was on his head. And he thought — Wait a minute, I'll bet I can get Mom to feel sorry for me, and she'll dip into the old man's pockets when he's asleep. And so he came dragging home in clothes that hadn't been washed in weeks. And his aged parents bailed him out. They drew his bathwater. They washed his clothes. And they barbecued up filet mignon. And do you know what the good son felt, when he came home from the fields and saw his evil brother getting the ticker-tape parade? *What am I, ground chuck?*

The good brother bided his time, and then went to the cops in the other country and turned his sorry brother in, took the reward, and invested it. And then, in a hostile takeover, he got control of his father's business. He sent his parents to a nice, clean nursing home where they had art therapy. And when the Prodigal Son was finally released from the hoosegow, he had to beg in the marketplace, until the Prodigal Son finally *died*. And the good son danced and danced. Happy ending!

Thank You So Much for Stopping
by Halley Feiffer

Ashleigh, an attractive young woman with a steely, unblinking gaze and a plastered smile on her face, is standing on the side of the road waving frantically at an approaching car. Although picture perfect in her outward appearance, there is a palpable anxiety bubbling inside her that suggests first appearances can be deceiving … and, in this case, deadly! What follows is a sardonic glimpse at a deeply troubled woman wrestling with personal demons while feigning cordiality and light-hearted humor in the face of having accidentally killed her husband. This ingenious character sketch poses some tantalizing questions about the aggrieved widow's self-delusion that remain unanswered.

ASHLEIGH: Hi, excuse me? Hi! *(Sound of the car slowing down and pulling up to her)* Hi, um. *(She makes a gesture for "please roll down your window." Sound of the window being rolled down. With a big smile, like the gracious hostess)* Hi! Thank you *so* much for stopping. I'm *so* sorry to bother you, I'm just having a *little* bit of a problem. I'd love your help. I'm *so* sorry, I *never* do this, it's just … *kind* of an emergency — oh no, don't worry, it's not the end of the world or anything. I'm fine, it's just — oh, this is so embarrassing — *(She chokes on her words; she is suddenly emotional.)* Oh, it's just so hard to ask for *help!* *(Beat. She collects herself quickly.)*

I'm sorry. I don't know what got into me. Excuse me. So, thank you so much for stopping and here's the thing: I just, as I was driving — I'm going over to my mother's house — *(Points to her car in the distance.)* — Yup that's me, right over there, the Prius, uh-huh — so, as I was driving, I just …

Accidentally killed my husband. *(Grimaces.)* I know, it's *so* embarrassing, I just —

(Suddenly remembers something.) Oh! My gosh, I can't believe it. I forgot to introduce myself. I'm so sorry, how rude. *(Sticking out her hand)* I'm Ashleigh, what's your name? Susan? That's my *mother's* name! No I am not kidding, it really is! And what's your name? Jerry?

That's my *brother's* name! No, don't get too excited, Jerry, I was kidding that time. *(Laughs loudly at her own joke.)* So *anyway:* I just killed my husband, and I was wondering if you guys —

Oh, well that's a good question. I'm sorry, I should've explained that right away. What happened was, we were driving over to my mother's house — I said that — and we were just sort of joking around, and he was, you know, joshing with me about how bad a driver I am, and I got kind of peeved, 'cause — well, I don't know why, I'm usually very even-tempered, but things have been sort of tough lately — *(Gets sort of emotional again, tries not to let it show)* — and anyway I got sort of peeved, and I said: "Well, if you hate the way I drive so much, why don't you get out of the car?" and he said: "Maybe I will" and I said, "Good, then do that," and I pulled over, and he got out, and then, as a joke, sort of, I sort of pretended to, like, you know, hit him with the car. But here's the thing: I actually *am* a pretty bad driver, and here's the thing: I *did* hit him, and I definitely didn't *mean* to, but then I thought, well hey, people get hit by cars all the time. I didn't hit him that hard, I'm sure I didn't do any serious damage, but here's the thing: I did. *(Grimaces.)* Yeeeeah. You know, it's the sort of thing that could happen to anyone, but when it happens to you, you're like, *aaaah, what do I do?* You know? So what I'm *wondering* is: Would you guys mind if I just kind of *loaded* him into your backseat, and we could just drive him over to the hospital real quick? It'll just be real quick — I have to be somewhere myself in half an hour.

I'm sorry? Oh, well I can't very well put him in *my* backseat, I've got both the kids back there. Yeeeeah, I do, two little ones. Little Susan and Little Jerry! No, just kidding, those aren't their names. But that reminds me actually — and I hate to be needy — but do you guys have any babysitting experience? I'm so sorry. I hate to be needy, but as I said, things *have* been sort of tough lately, and — *(Sound of the car pulling away)* Oh no, wait what? Oh no no no wait, don't — what are you — *what?*

Bridewell

by Charles Evered

Kristen, an emotionally overwhelmed college student, slowly comes to terms with a breath-stopping exorcism of the guilt and remorse that has plagued her since childhood: food issues. Here she recalls an unsettling incident she experienced as an adolescent in a passionate exchange with her sorority sisters. Kristen's absorbing examination of her obsession with weight is a poignant self-portrait of a young girl's struggle to reconcile the inescapable guilt of her addiction while sinking deeper into tearful, defeated despair.

KRISTEN: Look, just be glad you're not me. Maybe I do have a little issue with food. I remember when a certain someone *ripped my heart out*. It was my total low point. I was going to those Overeaters Anonymous meetings with my mother — which is kind of ironic, because she's the person who used to shove food in my face all the time anyway. It's kind of like going to a Serial Killer's Anonymous meeting and having Ted Bundy drive you there. So, this certain someone *dumps* me, and as my mother is driving us home, it's like, what do ya know, she just happens to stop at a Rite Aid, and out she comes with a ten-pound box of candy, and all I remember after that was seeing our twenty pudgy little fingers pulling and twisting and gouging out the candies and me just shoving them into my mouth, and that's when I got this great idea: "I won't eat them," I thought. I'll just chew them. If I chew them without swallowing, then I never will have eaten them at all. And all of this will have been nothing but a bad dream. So I put like fourteen of them in my mouth and I just *chomped,* but without swallowing, feeling all the chocolaty juices sliding down my throat and my brain flooding with endorphins and after about eight minutes, I hacked it up in a napkin and calmly put it on the dashboard and repeated the process over and over until all the candy was gone. Would that qualify as a "food issue," would you say?

A Preface to the Alien Garden
by Robert Alexander

In this visceral monologue from a "gangsta rap" full-length script, the author weaves a cautionary tale of young African Americans caught up in a swaggering gang lifestyle that glorifies greed, material consumption, and violence. But there is also a poetic note to the script voiced by tough-as-nails, seventeen-year-old Lisa in an almost apocalyptic fantasy vision that echoes the biblical book of Ezekiel, The Wizard of Oz, *and* Star Trek. *Here, Lisa — who believes she was abducted and held prisoner in a flying saucer while metal plates were inserted into her by aliens — is marking turf with her can of spray paint as she waits patiently for the mother ship to return so her quest for fulfillment will be rewarded.*

LISA: I'm a dream merchant. I've got dreams for sale — light beams for sale. This is the place to git in the space race, 'cause there are ninety-nine ways to git to Venus from here and thirty-nine ways to git to Mars. All you gotta do is click yo' heels together ... three times to catch a light beam ... *(Beat)* The other day, Zeke told me the facial markings of the Ibo tribe are also worn on the faces of other Ibo warriors — many galaxies away. He told me — a time will come — when all the other Ibo warriors throughout the universe will descend upon this land, to kill all thine enemies ... to return us to our rightful place. And those lost at birth — shall be found again.

Zeke also told me — that Monster Kody is the second coming of Malcolm X and one day he will rise from the lion's pit, he will throw off the chains that bind him, and he will lead us to the Promised Land, for it has already been written in the blood of the lamb. *(Beat)*

I was not meant to be earthbound. One day I'm gonna break gravity's hold on me. I was meant to be amongst the stars. I was meant to move with the speed of light. I was meant to move like the creatures I saw — among the creatures there was something that looked like a blazing torch — constantly moving. The fire would blaze up and shoot out flashes of lightning!

(Lights become harshly bright, creating the illusion of the light from a flying saucer.)

I just stood there, as the creatures darted back and forth with the speed of lightning. As I was looking at the four creatures — I saw four wheels of light — I saw four wheels touching the ground, one beside each of the creatures. All four wheels were alike — each shone like a precious stone. The rims of the wheels were covered with eyes. Whenever the creatures moved, the wheels moved with them. And when the creatures rose up from the earth — so did the wheels ... every time the creatures moved or stopped or rose in the air, the wheels did exactly the same. But when I looked into the light above their heads ... I saw it for the first time — a dome made of dazzling crystal — *the mother ship* — shone like a million dazzling lights.

Cinderella
by Chris Wind

Here is an original, ingenious version of the classic Cinderella story that adds an offbeat and yet refreshing view of the events so well known to all. This version, with all the familiar storyline loosely in place, is told by Cinderella's Sister in a very hip and knowing attitude. The fractured fairy tale world is by turns funny and satiric as the stepsister embarks on a candid recital of the perils and pitfalls of daily life with "poor little Cinderella" in this explosive parody.

CINDERELLA'S SISTER: Poor little Cinderella! Who more deserving of finding her prince and turning into a princess! Yeah, right!

First off, Cinderella did *not* have to do all the hardest work in the house. Our stepfather was a "man of rank," remember, and my mother no peasant. We had such fine rooms and beautiful clothes, and status enough to be invited to the King's ball. So we certainly had maids and servants to scrub the floors and wash the dishes. Cinderella *offered* to help with the work, probably because she had nothing else to do. She didn't seem interested in much besides pleasing people. Drove me crazy. And she did *not* have to sleep "in a straw bed in a poor room at the top of the house." Think her father would put up with that?

Certainly not. She had a good bedroom just like the rest of us.

The story goes that my sister and I were proud. True enough. What's wrong with that? What's wrong with being proud of what you can do, of what you've worked hard at to learn well? All those fine clothes people kept talking about were of my sister's making — she was into fashion design. And as for me, well, it was known I could ride a horse to win most competitions in the land. So sure we were proud. But vain? Yes, we spent a lot of time in front of that full-length mirror. My sister had to see the effect of her creations — and so I suppose she's as vain as one gets to be in that line of work — and as a favor, especially on days too wet or too cold for the horses to be out, I often modeled her half-finished pieces for her. But that's it. I wasn't even good-looking by contemporary standards. No peaches and cream in my complexion!

And it's true, Cinderella wasn't invited to the ball. But only because the King thought she was too young. And we certainly didn't snub her like you think. We called her into our rooms, and asked her for advice on our clothes to make her feel part of the excitement. She liked that. You know how younger sisters are, she wanted to iron this and mend that. We even let her do our hair.

But we *never* called her Cinder-wench, or actually, even Cinderella. Her nickname was Kinderella — little child — and somehow the "K" must have gotten changed to a "C." As for what happened at the ball, that's true too. She was very beautiful, our new little stepsister. We never denied that. And when beauty and wealth come together, most people fall over themselves like asses. Those at the ball were no different: to them, appearance is everything. My sister was stunned by Cinderella's gown; and she gawked, it's true. But out of professional interest, not jealousy as most people think. I wasn't jealous either — I just wanted to ride one of those impressive silver stallions she came with.

And as for that bit about the yellow dress, the story goes that Cinderella asked my sister if she could borrow it to wear at the next ball, and my sister said no way. Well, I don't know, that might have happened, I wasn't there. That yellow dress is one of her favorites, one of the first dresses she made. But I think that if my sister *had* said no, she would've offered another instead. Then again, Cinderella's tone can be so sweet and self-effacing sometimes, I can imagine my sister saying no out of sheer irritation and leaving it at that.

The rest of the story is pretty much accurate. All three of us went to the second ball, Cinderella forgot about her curfew, lost her slipper on the way out, and — there is one thing I want to set straight though: I did *not* try on the glass slipper. Quite apart from the fact that I didn't want to marry that prince — or any prince, or anyone at all, actually — a glass slipper? You've got to be kidding. That'd be worse than wearing high heels. Not only would it make walking difficult, but with the obvious risk of broken glass — cutting, embedding — it would discourage movement altogether. No thank you! But as I said to Cinderella, if the shoe fits, wear it. And we *all* will live happily ever after.

My Battle with Bulimia
by Peter Langman

Julie — a shy and sensitive young woman suffering from bulimia, an eating disorder that has become her personal demon — explores the contradictions in herself as she seeks self-forgiveness and a renewed sense of purpose in life. This dark and yet poignant original monologue voices her struggle for redemption from an addiction that has been the cause of intense personal suffering and estrangement from society. But guilt and fear cannot be laughed away, and as the fine line between addiction and potential death grows thinner, we are left to question if Julie's world of buried secrets and abandoned dreams will finally spiral out of control.

JULIE: My body makes me crazy. I just want to look acceptable, but there's no controlling it. I diet, but the weight comes back. I purge, but the weight stays the same. Laxatives, diuretics — nothing works on me. I'm a mess! A failure! Can't I do anything right? Ever since I was a kid — all the wrong curves in all the wrong places. It's one long humiliation.

Food is my necessary poison. You can't live without it, so it's necessary. But it poisons my life. It poisons my relationship with myself. It ruins everything. It wasn't supposed to become a habit. I promised myself it wouldn't become a habit. Just something to get me through a rough spot — a quick way of dropping a few pounds. That's all. That's all it was supposed to be. The whole point of throwing up was to help me lead a better life — make my boyfriend happy, have friends, be confident about getting involved in clubs and teams and things. But it got to a point where I realized my entire life had vanished, and the only thing I looked forward to was stuffing myself and vomiting. Planning the binge — what to eat, where to get it, when I could do it, and then the horrible glory of the purge. Help me lead a better life? It has become my life. All I wanted was to be a little thinner so I'd be noticed.

You want to know how messed up I am? OK. I'm so happy that my boyfriend is nice to me now that I've lost weight, and I hate him for not loving me as I was and pushing me into bulimia. Will I leave him? Are you crazy? He finally likes me. I'd die if he left me. How messed up is that?

I feel gross and disgusting and guilty and shameful for what I do, but I'm thrilled that I've found a way to eat and still keep my weight down. How messed up is that? Sometimes I want people to notice me and say I'm pretty, but other times I just want to disappear and never be noticed again. I want to be in love with someone, be accepted, be understood, but then I think that I really don't need or want anyone. Sometimes I want to have guys interested in me, but other times the thought of someone being close to me and touching my body makes me almost sick. How messed up is that?

I wanted to keep my bulimia a secret, but then I was so mad that no one even seemed to care enough to notice that I was in hell. Then I realized that I want my parents to know so they can help me through this, but I do everything I can to keep them from ever finding out. How messed up is that?

Last week I was at a funeral. My cousin's. My cousin Cassandra. Cassie was only a couple years older than me. We practically grew up together. And there she was — laid out in a casket. I never even knew she had an eating disorder. And all I kept thinking was, "Oh, my God. Oh, my God." She's gone. There she is, but she's gone. Why didn't she tell me? Didn't she know I was going through the same thing? But then, why didn't I tell her? We always acted so happy — but we were both going through hell. Her family knew. I found out she had been in and out of the hospital. But her parents never told me. They kept it a secret. They were embarrassed. But maybe we could have helped each other. I don't know how, but there must have been something we could have done. Just knowing that about each other might have changed everything. I couldn't watch when they lowered the coffin into the grave — not Cassie — so young, so alive. How could she be dead? Cassie, Cassie. What happened to you? What's happening to me?

Mom? Dad? I need to talk to you. Well, I've been wanting to tell you something for a while — no, I'm not pregnant. No — I'm not doing drugs. I'm sorry for getting you all worked up and worried, but — well, you know what happened to Cassie? I'm kind of having the same issues. Don't freak out — please. Just listen. I need help. I need you to help me through this. I don't want to die.

Glass Eels
by Nell Leyshon

Lily, a troubled and emotionally fragile young girl whose family runs a mortuary business in an austere and stultifying rural community, is struggling to confront an internal conflict with spirituality and her emerging sexuality. Late at night, Lily is inevitably drawn to the river where her mother mysteriously died and where thousands of eels are now stirring as they anticipate their solitary migration to the sea. There she meets Kenneth, an older family friend to whom she is attracted, and recalls a harrowing memory of the unfathomable cruelty adults are capable of visiting on children. (Note: The symbolic title suggests the sexual energy of eels that are poised to stir from the silt, mate, and return to the sea.)

LILY: I think I'm like my mother.
She came down here at night.
I know I shouldn't come, but I can't help myself.
I know she came here. Sat here. Swam in there.
She's not in the house anymore.
I used to look for her. I found things she touched. I found a
piece of paper with her handwriting. I found a shoe in the garden.

A dress she'd worn.
It hadn't been washed.
(LILY sits up.)
I want to tell you this thing. But I don't want you to look at me.
Look away. That's it.
If you look at me I'll stop.
I used to think everyone had dead bodies in their homes. I'd
go to the room where he got them ready. He caught me one day,
looking at the powder he used on their skin to tighten it.
I was gonna use it on me but he took it away from me, said it was
only for dead skin.
I started going down at night and if we had one in I'd lift the
sheet from their faces.
I used to think if I looked at them long enough I could bring
them back to life, make them breathe again.
One night there was a new one there. I took the sheet and
peeled it down. Stood and stared.
It was my mother.
(Kenneth looks.)
No. Don't look at me.
It had happened late at night and no one had woken me to tell
me. That's how I found out.
Her skin was streaked with mud. Her hair still damp from the
river. A piece of weed in it.
(Pause)
I stood there and tried to make her breathe again. Tried to
make her chest move.
Nothing happened.
So I reached out and pulled her eyelids up, to get her to open
her eyes and look at me. But her eyes had rolled back and
there was just the whites.
I tried to pull the lids back down but they had stuck.
I had to go upstairs and into my dad's room. I had to tell him
to come with me, to see what I'd done.
He followed me down and I showed him.
He saw and then he turned and grabbed my arm, too tight. He
shook me and screamed at me, told me I shouldn't have gone in.

And then he hit me. Here. *(Touches face.)*
Some things that happen to you, you get them in here.
(Touching head) And you can't get them out.
I wish you could take it out so I didn't have to remember it.

PEACHES

by Cristal Chanelle Truscott

Inspired in part by Nina Simone's classic song, "Four Women," PEACHES *examines archetypes of African American female attitudes and identities spanning time, from slavery to the present day. The journeys of the resilient young slave, jazz diva, club-goer, romantic, revolutionary, and single mother are voiced by multiple "Peaches" in these historical periods and is a startling, highly original metaphor that illuminates the emotional complexity of those who may, at any given time, be reduced to being called an "angry black woman." Evocative, inspiring, and stirring,* PEACHES *resurrects the memory, truth, and perception of African American women who have marched triumphantly to their own drummer for centuries.*

PEACHES: I need me a man with some color. That's what I tell myself. So I started dating a Nigerian. He showed me pictures of his sisters and said I reminded him of the girls back home. Later, though, I realized he was crazy. He kept comparing me to his last girlfriend who was White, and that was it for me. I can't see what he could possibly want with me, all the while reminding me of how I'm so much more "difficult" than his last girlfriend. And then I remembered that nearly all of Africa has been carved up, placed under colonial rule, and infected with the same Eurocentric crap that we have to deal with. And I understood why the brother was crazy.

Sometimes, I think about Africa and I know that with all the colonization that has terrorized the land, it's not half the dreamland I want it to be. But, I still think of it that way. I dream to myself, *If I was there, I could feel beautiful.* I've spent hours in front of the mirror telling myself, "Black is beautiful, girl. Girl, Black is beautiful. Black is beautiful, girl. Girl, Black is beautiful, and you such a pretty Black girl." Yet, if Black is so beautiful, why is it such a fight for me to believe it. I mean, if I had pitch-black skin and pinch-short hair — would I be noticed at all? When they colonized the Africans, they really did a thorough job. I used to dream about Africa as being the homeland. But now I think, why would I want to go there only to deal with another version of the same baggage I grew up with? The slave mentality, the colonized mentality — what's the difference?

Elephant
by Margie Stokley

Michelle, a broken-hearted and sensitive teenager, is experiencing the painful emptiness and loss of her older brother, Jay, a Marine in his twenties who recently died in a tragic car accident. While struggling to bear her unbearable grief and sense of loss, Michelle has been seeing a therapist — apparently ineffectually — and is now confined to a hospital where she obsessively overapplies makeup and lashes out at the world while battling her frustration. Here, Michelle introduces herself at a group therapy session and we catch a fleeting glimpse of her sardonic humor that's almost always tinged with sadness.

MICHELLE: Hi. My name is Michelle. *(She does a crazy gesture and noise that somehow mocks suicide.)* Just kidding. No, really — thrilled to be here. What do you want to know? What do you want me to say ... *(Silence)*

Oh, wait, that's right. This is not a conversation — it's a session. This is my time to share, with *complete strangers,* how I feel ... Well, I feel like talking about trees. How do you feel about them? Wait. Please, don't speak ... let me. My fascination *stems* from this one tree. *(She silently mouths "stems" again to emphasize the irony.)* Rough crowd. *(Pause)* Well, it's gigantic and right outside my bedroom window. Some nights I feel like it wants in. Wants in to my perfect pink and white striped room. My room is perfect, not because it's everything I want. It's just perfectly planned, the pillows, the balloon shades, the pictures, the bed, the window seat, my stuffed animals. I have even more animals under my bed. I have guilt about suffocating them ... I feel, it doesn't matter. They don't match. *(Pause)* They really don't. Well, it can't fall now because I just predicted it. What you think is going to happen — never does. It's a relief. You can't know it all. I just feel like in *my movie* that's what will happen. There'll be a huge thunderstorm with lightning, my tree will explode, and I'll be crushed. I can see myself split in half. I don't want to be surrounded by all those people who would need to be there if I got crushed. I am over groups. No offense.

Samantha
by Sofia Dubrawsky

Samantha, a feisty young girl in her early teens with sparkling wit and theatrical flair, is president of her school's Girls Club, and when we meet her in this original monologue, she is standing in front of a chatty group of club members at an after-school meeting. Although the club members pride themselves on practicing democracy and open discussion at their meetings, the first — and last — order of business is gossip and a review of the latest school rumors. Samantha's agenda, however, is quite transparent here, and it will not be killing any suspense to reveal that it involves the handsome new boy in school.

SAMANTHA: Girls Club is now in session. I am the President this week so what I say goes — and right now I'd like everyone to shut up! *(SAMANTHA darts a few evil glances until the group is silent.)* Thank you. First order of business, we all know everyone is talking about Katie's party: who kissed who, who didn't kiss who, and who was crying in the bathroom over it. It's time to stop spreading the rumors around school that I kissed Toby, when obviously I did not because Toby is "definition disgusting" and he smells like butt-foot! If anyone in the club hears anyone say that I kissed him, tell them it's not true! As a member of this club, under Rule Number 32, titled "Rumor Control," it's your duty to keep all members' reputations in check. Furthermore, if anyone finds out who started this nasty rumor, please bring him or her to our "community court day." I'd like to lawyer-up for this one!

Next order of business: Blake. Blake kissed two different girls at the party, and I think we all know the first one was Jennifer Tyson. Then after Jennifer's mom picked her up early around 10:00 p.m., he was seen giving "sloppy seconds" to Tracey Fillmore by 10:45 p.m. *(She smiles.)* They were dancing and I totally saw them. She was all over him! OK, even though he is "Blake" and we have voted him "cutest new guy," he obviously can't get away with this. Raise your hand if you agree. *(She counts.)* OK, it's the majority. We must proceed with action. Personally, I've been thinking a lot about Blake, and since he's new, it's like he thinks he can just do whatever he wants. He needs someone to set him straight, someone who is established, popular, and a little bit shorter than him. It doesn't even have to be Jessica or Tracey. I don't think either are "Blake material" anyway. It could be someone totally different, like me for example? That would kill the Toby rumor. Raise your hand if you think Blake and I would make a cute couple. *(She counts.)* Excellent! Another majority! So the plan is, after club, he will be in the cafeteria getting out of Beat Boxing Club. That's when we'll corner him, and tell him that he should go out with me. It's really his only option after what he did on Saturday. His reputation needs cleansing. Remember: When you control the rumors, you control the school — and let's face it, we've got him wrapped around our pinkie toes.

That's all the proceedings for today. Now, let's get to work on our quilt squares.

Laughing Wild
by Christopher Durang

This classic madcap monologue by 2013 Tony Award winner Christipher Druang offers a satirical view of Thomas Gray's poem "Ode on a Distant Prospect of Eton College" and comically distorts the poet's vision of "moody madness laughing wild amid severest woe." Here, a Woman invites us to enter her chaotic dream world and we catch a disturbing glimpse of a hilarious, strange, and quite mad character overwhelmed by the perils of modern life in urban America. Although the Woman's frantic search for roots and purpose in an often purposeless world strikes a serious tone, it is her thwarted dreams and frustrated sense of reality that brings a frisky and often hilarious sense of comedic wit to the character portrait.

WOMAN: My favorite book is *Bleak House*. Not the book, but the title. I haven't read the book. I've read the title. The title sounds the way I feel. And my most recent accomplishment was getting up out of the gutter after I fell down leaving that crazy taxi driver. And my Scotch is Dewar's White Label.

I feel terribly sorry for my doctors. My doctors get exhausted listening to me. I can tell they feel my words are charging out of my mouth and trying to invade their brain cells, and they're frightened. Understandably. And that's why I try to practice being quiet from time to time. Let me be quiet for a second again. *(She is quiet.)* You see, you need that rest too, don't you?

Here is the key to existence. Are you all listening? Here is the key to existence; when I tell you this, you will know how to run your lives. You will know if you have been living life to the full, and if you realize you haven't been, you will know immediately how to correct that state of affairs. As soon as I tell you the key to existence. Are you ready? Are you ready for me to tell you?

Oh, dear, I've built it up too much, and it's really not all that significant. But it's what I got from the EST training: *Always breathe.* That's the basis of life, breathing. That's basically the basis. If you don't breathe, you die. *(Pause)* Well, it seemed more impressive when you hadn't slept for two days. If you're rested, it doesn't sound so important, but I try to hold on to it. The other major thing I learned is … *(Sincerely)* Well, I've forgotten it, so it couldn't have been too significant.

Well, then, I've covered everything I intended to. Thank you for giving me your attention. Good-bye, I love you. Of course, that's a lie. Some of you I think are first-class fools, and I hate you. In fact, I probably don't like any of you. Curse you! I curse all of you! May your children have webbed feet, and all your house pets get mange and worms!

I'm terribly sorry. I really can't leave you that way. The management would be so cranky if I cursed the audience right at the end of my speech, so forget I said that. I do love you. M-wah! I want to be a responsible member of this society, so give me a job if you can. I'm sure I can do *some*thing. I love you, m-wah! The ushers will give you my phone number, and the box office will field any job offers you call in. Thank you. Good-bye. Laugh laugh laugh laugh — I'm getting too tired to do the real laugh right now. Laugh laugh laugh. Laughing is a tonic. So forget crying. Cry, and you cry alone. Laugh and you … cry alone later. And remember — always breathe.

CHAPTER 4
A TIME OF INDEPENDENCE

"I am no bird, and no net ensnares me.
I am a free human being with an independent will."
— Charlotte Bronte, *Jane Eyre*

These heroic idylls to a time of independence provide a microcosmic portrait of nonconformists, freethinkers, and rebels who are capable of standing alone when challenged to the breaking point or forced to face the slings and arrows hurled by others with die-hard optimism. There is a cold-eyed sharpness here that is unfashionably persuasive in the characters' incessant search for answers to life's big questions. These combative figures have learned a great deal about despair, failed romances, and unfulfilled dreams, but are determined not to accept the painful or pathetic truths of life.

The authors sketch a portrait gallery of robust characters that reveal their fears, hopes, and passions while fiercely clinging to their independence. There is an indomitable willpower in the characters' valiant struggle to face the unbearable cruelty of life, scratch away the edgy surface of false hope, or confront the unutterable sadness of failed relationships. There is also a Renoir-like depth and shimmer to these portraits, as if the characters had stepped through the master painter's frame to voice their deeply felt emotions.

At times, there is an occasional note of sadness and despair when the spirit of independence is shattered by the intrusion of the outside world and the characters must distinguish the agonizing difference between illusion and reality. Even so, there is inevitably a note of hope that soothes the pain of remembrances of things past. What remains is to look honestly at the way the world *is,* not the way we may wish it to be.

Soda Fountain
by Richard Lay

Ma, a distraught and heartbroken woman, is grieving over the recent death of her young son, Francis, who drowned in a tragic accident. She tells a rather grim but insightful story of how she had come to love this child who was born less than perfect. The scarred memories, however, do little to comfort her in this unflinching portrait of the unhappy accident and the terrible ravages of time. Here, Ma tries to cope with her loss by voicing newfound strength and bittersweet resolve to exorcise the ghosts of the past.

MA: *(Looking into the distance)* When Francis was three I wanted to kill him because I knew he was ... you know, a dime or two short. I thought I couldn't love an idiot. And I proved myself so wrong ... he gave me strength as he struggled though all his humiliations at school. They spat at him, threw rocks at him, said terrible things. But through all of it he remained a constant, cheerful kid. He knew more about affection than anybody I know. He had an instinct about it. He knew that if I was worried, all he had to do was put his arms around me and kiss me. He knew that if I cried — all he had to do was smile. The warmth of our bodies meant everything. His father tried to pretend his son didn't exist in the later years. Jim thought that somehow he had failed.

The worst thing about death is visiting graves ... a mound of earth, flowers real or plastic, and the thought that the person you love is six feet down and rotting. It's difficult to comprehend that the person you loved so much will be a skeleton. It's difficult to love a dead person ... but I guess we want everybody to love us when we die.

Crispy Leaves
by Tara Meddaugh

Lexy, a meek and quite ordinary young woman, experiences a coming-of-age moment when she has a physical altercation with a florist that enables her to break free from the suffocating influence of her deceased mother. This original monologue offers an unflinching look at a young woman breaking free from the restraints imposed by a controlling parent and finally facing the consequences of choices made long ago ... but vowing to move forward with a renewed sense of purpose and strength.

LEXY: Yes, the tulips are dead, Mother. But I didn't originally plan that. Plan on giving you brown tulips. With crispy leaves. I tried to refuse them, but ... I'm just not good at talking with florists. But I know it's important to you — to have fresh flowers on your grave. So this afternoon — when she — the florist — when she brings out these dead ones, I try to explain. But still be polite, like you taught me. So I say, "Ma'am, thank you for the thought, but — " And I put my hand out, I gesture, to sort of make my point. And I'm not done, but that's all I get out, when she shoves them in my hand and almost screams at me, "You're welcome."

So the flowers are in my hands and she's looking at me, grinning, like she expects money or something. And I'm about to pay her. I'm about to pay her for four dead tulips and leave — when something — I don't know, something suddenly surges through me, through my veins — like I've got new blood in me! Powerful blood! Strong blood that people will listen to! Respect! So with my new blood pumping through me, I grab the tulips with one hand and this lady's neck with the other, and I shove those moldy flowers all over her! I shove them in her ears, and her mouth — since she's got it open, screaming — and just all over her face! And it feels good, Mother! It feels so good ...

Then I look back over at the brown tulips and I wonder if they're all really dead? And I want them now. So I let go of the woman and I cut off a little piece of blue ribbon from the counter, and I tie it around the flowers. And I come here. To you. And I know you're used to getting fresh flowers every day, but I want you to know that I'm not coming back tomorrow. Or the next day either. Because it's a two-hour bus ride to get here, and I have a job now. So you can have these dead flowers, Mother. But I'm keeping this tulip. Because it still has a little green in its stem.

I'll see you at Easter.

Ayravana Flies, or A Pretty Dish
by Sheila Callaghan

This satiric and absurd spoof of the avant-garde features the bubbling Olivia, a frizzy-haired, nutty-looking waitress with too-red lipstick and bulgy omnivorous eyes, who has just rediscovered her lost talent for exotic cooking. Here, she serves up a tasty monologue rich in bucolic humor and well-seasoned with joviality that provides plenty of spicy laughs. Olivia's "love song" to cooking blends moments of hilarity and self-effacing humor with a magical sense of hope and renewal as well.

OLIVIA: *So.* Chop chop chop I go, dice dice dice chop, mix mix, taste, mix mix sprinkle sprinkle pour, mix mix taste, cook cook cook cook cook taste sprinkle cook cook cook cook taste scream swear, cook cook cook cook cook cook taste and smile. And I'm shuttled to another time and place, growing up as a little girl on the vegetable farm. No. Yes, the vegetable farm. In my Tom Sawyer overalls and my straw hat and my bare feet, skipping through the plantation and digging up vegetables from the warm soil, then skipping home with a full basket and cooking them all up in a big wicker pot, then adding special spices I'd ordered from my spice catalogue, exotic spices with names too long to pronounce, from countries too small to see, and I'd serve them warm in a loaf of bread with the heart torn out.

Ooooh. Mmmmm. La la la la la. People clamored at my kitchen window in frenzied hordes for a taste of my wildly original dishes. "Olivia is cooking in her wicker pot again, bring the tin foil and the toothpicks!" Tearing each other's hair, ripping their own shirts. For a *taste*, I tell you. And after one bite they'd drop to the dirt in a swoon.

Because I made more than just dishes. I made *voodoo*. Not the creepy kind with the mumbling and the eyes rolled back and the rag doll stuck with pins. The good kind. I burned flavors into people's mouths — memories. I could conjure music from the tip of the tongue to the uvula, each tiny increment of space resounding a different chord. It was clear I had a future as a Voodoo Priestess of Culinary Wizardry. But alas. I got thwarted somewhere between point A and point A. Until now.

This Will Not Look Good on My Resume
by Jass Richards

Brett, a sharp-tongued young woman with a spirit of madcap adventure, embraces life's challenges with reckless abandon and the courage of a fearless warrior. In the following two monologues, she offers her tart and testy personal observations on the job application process and recalls one in a long line of jobs from which she has been unceremoniously fired. In the process, she paints a delicious portrait of employers and provides a wealth of thought-provoking hints for job seekers to consider when navigating the job market.

"The Application and Interview"

BRETT: A week later, just in time for income tax season, I was qualified to do personal income tax returns. But despite passing the course with flying colors, I almost didn't get hired. I failed the application form.

Name: I like it that this question comes first. It's one I can answer.

Address: I also know where I live.

Phone Number: Three for three!

Sex: Other.

Marital Status: No — Unmarried women have no status.

Name Known to References if Different from Name Indicated Above: Loud Mouth — At this point, I began to feel my application form advantage slipping away.

Education: Yes.

Scholastic Awards: Regional Math Quizmaster. Trout Township, 1972.

Employment History: Yes.

Attach additional page if necessary: No.

I'm not doing that anymore. I used to make out a complete list of all my previous jobs and attach it as directed. I thought I was displaying versatility and a wealth of experience. A friend — OK, an acquaintance — pointed out that I was displaying stupidity. With a list like mine, she said, I'd be considered a flight risk, a bad investment. Employers wanted someone who could hold down a job for more than — she scanned my neatly typed list — a week.

What aspect of your previous employment did you enjoy the most: Recess.

What aspect of your previous employment did you find the most challenging: Dealing with a moron supervisor.

Describe any skills or experience relevant to to the position applied for: Attention to to detail.

Hobbies: Snow shoveling, apparently — It had been a very long winter.

Have you ever lied: Yes. This answer is a lie.

Have you ever stolen anything from your previous employers: Yes. But only when my name was Heinz and my mother would have died otherwise.

Position applied for: Income Tax Filler-Outer.

Other kinds of work you might be interested in: Ship's Philosopher on the Starship Enterprise.

When I went for my final interview, I had a sneaking suspicion that the manager had read my application form, decided not to hire me, and then prepared the perfect list of interview questions to justify his decision. Not exactly standard procedure, but then he probably had the word "discretion" in his job description. And he intended to use it. After all, he'd certainly been to enough management training seminars. He couldn't wait to start the interview, and was practically grinning as he asked his first question. "Well, yes," I answered, "actually I *do* have experience working with the criminally insane."

"Brett at 602"

BRETT: My first job was in an office. I hated it. No, that's not true. Actually, I liked the job. It was the people I hated. Thus from the start,

I was destined for a long line of jobs in the "people professions."

Perhaps the most notable of these was my job at 602, a residential program run by the Mental Health Association. Selected patients from the local psych hospital — those with potential! — were transferred at some point in time to 602 — so called because its address was 602 Bonkers Street — where the staff would teach the residents life skills, help them find a job and an apartment, and generally provide support during their transition from institutionalized living to independent living. I highly recommend the program to those who work in an office.

I was hired as a relief worker and mostly covered the midnight shift. Which meant that I helped the residents make the transition from sleeping in a bed to sleeping in a bed. Which was OK because I would've had trouble teaching life skills. How to buy groceries, how to keep track of your checking account — these were adult skills we were dealing with, and I had neither the desire nor the need to infantilize them. After all, people who need people are, well, codependent.

Besides, you want *life* skills? OK, how about how we deal with the recognition that you're never really going to amount to much. And how to be content nevertheless. And, yes, how to make foil headgear that is durable yet fashionable.

On my first midnight shift, I took Kessie with me, partly thinking of all those sweet and cuddly animal therapy programs — and partly thinking that if I dozed off, she'd be my alarm system, sure to wake up growling the second any crazy with a knife walked into the room. Turned out she refused to go to sleep. I stretched out on the couch and she sat on my head. All night. At full alert. Apparently ready to scream. The place scared her. No wonder. All of my coworkers had previous experience with mental illness. First-hand. In fact, I think that was a prerequisite for obtaining a full-time position. A relapse seemed to be the prerequisite for promotion.

Stupid
by Kevin Six

Miram, a precocious and ingenious young girl with a crisp, sharp wit and penetrating insight, simply thinks that she is too smart for her mother, adults, or the world at large to understand and offers a sobering portrait of teenagers in our time. This richly warm, clear-eyed character sketch is alternately comic and satiric by turns. It is also liberally laced with serious, thought-provoking issues of youthful optimism and hope in conflict, with despair and disillusionment that address the changing nature of society and is sure to speak to listeners of all ages.

MIRAM: Boys are stupid! Teachers, for the most part, are stupid too. My mom's stupid, but that goes without saying. Not everybody is stupid. I don't want you to think that I'm some dour teenager who hates the world and thinks everyone is stupid for no apparent reason. No, I'm a dour teenager who hates much of the world and thinks a number of people are stupid for very specific reasons.

Take Jimmy Dean. My mom thinks it's just hilarious that I know a boy named Jimmy Dean and won't take anything I say about him seriously. I don't really know why and she won't explain — she just chokes on her Entenmann's Danish and laughs until I leave the breakfast table. Jimmy Dean is stupid for a very specific reason. And that reason is that he used to like me and now he hates me. Or, he hasn't grown out of pulling my hair and kicking me like he did when we were little to show me he liked me. No. Now he says mean things about me. To my face! And it confuses me. And I hate it when I'm confused over a stupid boy.

My teachers are stupid, just like my mom is, because they can't remember back to their teenage years. Or because they've seen too many teenagers' problems and are just desensitized to them. Or is it that they do remember their teenage years but were worse than me? Either way, where's the compassion? Where's the hope in a new generation? I mean, isn't it enough that they're leaving us with a planet that is in desperate need of resuscitation? That they're leaving a banking system in shambles? A national debt that I can't calculate and I take calculus? That they're sitting back and just letting a war machine run the government and maybe soon the world? A war machine, mind you, that will draft me thanks to that stupid feminism thing my mom talks so reverently about.

What were the gains of feminism again? Women can vote, still don't earn fair wages, can't keep a job after getting pregnant unless they sue and now can go to war and die for a country that is so screwed up that we can't fix it. And we will probably have to go to war. Me and Jimmy Dean and any of my friends who are stupid enough to go to war or worse — to get drafted — for people who don't even understand us! Yeah, boys are stupid but they have redeeming qualities. Adults ... Politicians ... Sheep ... are stupid, and I think it's time I did something about it. I can't wait until I get to vote. I just hope it's not too late.

In the Cards
by Caroline Russell-King

Rivka, a sensitive and perceptive young girl with a vivid imagination, is a psychic who foresees her marriage to a childhood sweetheart at the age of five, shadows him for years, and then abandons him at the altar when she has a disturbing vision of him with another woman. Now, she has reluctantly acknowledged the spirit and adventure of the unknown shadow world, embracing whatever destiny each day may hold for her. Rivka offers a lighthearted and yet unflinching look at her early childhood and the sometimes comic consequences of her psychic gift that is both funny and painful at the same time.

RIVKA: I know what some of you are thinking. Is she the psychic? She doesn't look like a psychic. Surprise! I wasn't born one though. My childhood was hell. My mother was psychic. The only good thing was she was the only mother on the block who never asked me where I was going, who I was seeing, or what time I'd be home. They say mothers have eyes in the back of their heads. My mother's eyes used to be in the back of my head, on the inside. Most mothers read romance novels for

fun — my mother read the neighbor's minds. She used t
things I was *going* to do. When I was seven, I got gr
weeks for something she said I was going to do in the back seat of a
bus when I was sixteen. Most kids get punished for things they said, I
got punished for things I thought. She threatened to wash my brain out
with soap. I'd be terrified she'd do it one day and bubbles would come
out of my ears at school.

Anyway, my life changed when my friend Daisy found a package of
cigarettes on the street, and we decided to climb a tree and smoked
them all. I got dizzy, fell out of the tree — that's when I learned
smoking is hazardous to your health. Daisy got really scared because
I'd hit my head and was unconscious and so she ran to tell my mother,
which was redundant because she already knew. I wasn't out for very
long, but when I came 'round I found I had the curse too. No, not that.
That didn't happen until I was thirteen. The psychic curse. At age five,
I got even with my mother. We never really discussed it, but she knew.
All I had to do was gasp, or giggle at the appropriate time and watch
her cringe. Growing up I found out all sorts of things a child shouldn't
know. My mother lusted after Frank, our grocer. My dad fiddled his
books, my aunt drank, the minister wore women's underwear. Life isn't
pretty when you're psychic, but it sure is colorful!

God in Bed
by Glenn Alterman

*This original monologue paints an affectionate portrait of the
adorable Joanna, a shopaholic young woman who leaves a trail of
comic carnage in her wake. A certified bargain basement butterfly,
Joanna dispenses a good deal of insider's dope on shopping strategies
and offers a handy shopper's guide to selecting markdown brands of
clothing. In this nonstop roller coaster of rapier wit and wisdom,
Joanna teems with joy as she recalls a recent shopping expedition that
fulfilled her most cherished bargain basement dreams and wishes.*

JOANNA: I see that word, *"Sale, sale!"* and lose all sense of
everything! My knees buckle, my hands start sweating. Everything in

me says, *"Don't, don't,"* but I *do* enter, stand in the doorway. I know, I mean, I *know* I should walk away, but Bali Hai calls. And soon I fall down a wishing well into a land of magical markdowns. I'm drenched in a waterfall of "Last Day of Sale" signs. I start to grab things, fight with other customers. "I had that first! Get your own!" It's survival of the fittest, and I'm a pro!

Soon my pile of clothes becomes immense. I can't possibly carry all those clothes. I cry out! My guardian angel, a lovely saleswoman, floats down, touches my arm: "May I help you, young lady?" She sees my distress. I immediately cry out, "Yes! — Where's the fitting room?" And we start our trek to try-on heaven, but are stopped by the Nazi-like fitting room gatekeeper who says, "Sorry, you can only take in eight items at a time." "Eight. Eight? Why so few?" I say. Why not cut off an arm or leg? *Sophie's Choice* was small in comparison. How can I choose, how, which one first? The silk blouse, the Armani skirt? I agonize under her hateful eyes. She cruelly recounts each garment, then brands me with a bright colored number eight.

Finally, the fitting room. Four walls, a seat, and a mirror. I get undressed, look at myself, feel so unfinished; a naked caterpillar. Only new clothes can complete me. And as I try them on, I blossom into a bargain basement butterfly. The bigger the mark-down, the more I smile. And yes to this; and yes to that! My saleswoman dutifully waits outside my door. I rush to show her my choices. "Yes," she says. "That's lovely, dear." And I know she means it.

As I pirouette for her as I do for daddy, "Yes," she says. "That one too. That dress is — you." And I agree, it is me — but at fifty percent off! Soon, many of these lucky items will be taken home to my climate controlled, walk-in closet where they'll be hung on "only" wooden hangers, gently washed in Woolite or dry cleaned only when needed.

Then that last journey to the cash register. I almost cry as I see each mark-down fly by. I embrace my new clothes like third world orphans. Then, the final item, my sale complete. Shopping bags in hand, I lovingly wave good-bye to the entire staff of the store, who are now standing in the doorway, saluting and bidding me a tear-filled good-bye. "No, please, please don't cry. The Labor Day sales are only a few months away. Till then, kiss-kiss, adieu."

Something in the Air
by Richard Dresser

In this mildly gritty but lighthearted monologue, Sloane, an attractive but mysterious woman as sassy as she is seductive, is lecturing to Walker, a high-strung, down-on-his-luck loner who has fallen in love with Sloane while he is involved in an investment scheme to buy a terminally ill man's life insurance policy. Here, Sloane shares her philosophy about personal hygiene and paints an artful portrait of darkly serious and raucously funny views on, of all things, teeth!

SLOANE: The longest I ever went without seeing a dentist was three and a half years. The one I finally went to scared me half to death vis-à-vis periodontal issues, so I started with a Water Pik and baking soda, and I was brushing eight, ten, twenty times a day. Once I got over my hangup about brushing in public, there was really no reason to stop. My dentist gave me a little rubber hammer and I'd hit my gums three hundred times, five times a day, to toughen them up. Go ahead, feel my gums.

I know. The problem was, my teeth just got too important and started to take over my life. I had to cart all my dental equipment around wherever I went — did I mention I was sleeping around a lot back then? I didn't have a clue where I'd wake up — a bed, a car, a boat, off in some gravel pit. Upshot, I had a pretty falling-out with this dentist over third-party billing. My insurance company, or should I say my *ex*-insurance company — do you want all the details?

Oh, OK. So, long story short, I left that dentist and found this fabulous new dentist. She had a very relaxed, holistic approach to dental hygiene, so I got on a new program where my teeth are decaying at the same rate as the rest of me. We'll all go out together in a blaze of glory. And at long last I can live *with* my teeth and not *for* my teeth.

LUMP

by Leena Luther

LUMP: 19 Monologues from a 27-Year-Old Breast Cancer Survivor, *a sensitive collection of monologues that examine the ravages of breast cancer, chronicles the heroic and unflinching journey of a young woman — the author — with heartfelt emotion, passionate eloquence, and genuine honesty. In the following two monologues, the author paints an absorbing human portrait that reaffirms the power of courage over fear. Unspoken doubts and inevitable challenges are voiced with a seamless blend of humor, pathos, and emotion that offers a touching glimpse into the life of a courageous breast cancer survivor.*

"The Princess with the Pea"
LEENA: It feels like the princess was right to lose sleep over a pea. It may be small, but it's not supposed to be there.
Wouldn't it be funny, if this were all some sort of princess test? I can see the updated version now. It would be some Fox- or MTV-inspired reality show. Nine ladies, one pea. *Who* is the biggest princess? In a surprising twist, the pea is revealed to be a cancerous tumor. *Ahhhh!* Watch them all scream.
I think I may be acting more troll than princess though. Ask my family, they'll tell you I grunt a lot. And my cats won't leave my side, like little minions. Or is that more princess? Minions seem like something they should have too. And a dashing prince. I did go on a date last night, mostly to prove to myself that I still could. He was tall. He did have dark hair. And he did kiss me.
He was just being gallant though. He left to go on vacation to a far-away land, and I, the fair maiden he so chivalrously distracted, have an adventure of my own this morning. Surgery, the start of many adventures coming my way. I'm laying here in rags on an uncomfortable bed, waiting for them to put me under.
Heh. Waiting for the princess with the pea to turn into a sleeping beauty.

"The Fifth Annual 'Leena's Not Dead Party'"
LEENA: It was very right.
Well, OK, maybe a few people thought it was
kind of wrong. But I liked it. It's not every day your mom
hangs a homemade banner from the trees that says, "The
Fifth Annual Leena's Not Dead Party."
It was a good time. The party, I mean. And the not
being dead. The cancer that put me in this situation in the
first place — that was kind of wrong.
But hey, bygones are bygones, for the most part.
I'm hanging out in the woods next to the beach with fifty
or so of my closest friends and family. So what if I can't
play some pick-up volleyball because the ball impact will
make my arms swell up in some freaky cancer lymph node
thing. I was never good at volleyball anyway. I'll just have
a beer instead.
My new boyfriend is here. Isn't he cute? He's also
smart, and brave too. He's meeting my family for the first
time. No pressure. I'm sure lots of future husbands meet
their future wives' families at a "Not Dead" party. But, just in
case, don't tell him I said that. Just because he's "The One"
doesn't mean we don't have a very important dating
process to respect.
I'm trying to respect all the processes in my life
actually, and appreciate that not everything needs to be
perfect. I may not be positive of the outcome, but things
look pretty good. I've made it five years without a relapse.
And my boyfriend doesn't seem to be scared away by an
irreverent banner slogan.
So yeah, I'd say things are very right. They are just
as they should be.

Things of Dry Hours
by Naomi Wallace

Set in Birmingham, Alabama, in the heart of the Great Depression, this monologue features Cali — a sullen and resentful African-American woman who cuts firewood and washes sheets for white folks in the next town. A widow who lives with her unemployed Sunday school teacher father Tice — a member of the Communist Party — Cali scrambles and scrapes for work while being a captive audience for her father's Socialist rants. Her world is turned upside down, however, when her father agrees to offer shelter to Corbin Teel, a mysterious white factory worker on the run from the law.

There is an initial curious and unspoken attraction between Cali and Corbin that flows uneasily between racial tension and raw emotion. Later in the play, Cali, wearing her nightgown, slips quietly into the room where her father is asleep in his chair and begins to tear pages out of her father's large Bible while she voices what is preying on her conscience.

CALI: Forgive me, Father, for I have sinned. *(She tears out another page, but in short bursts so it tears differently.)* Twice so far. Here goes a third. *(She tears out a third page in a different manner from the other two.)* That's a kinder music. Lord. He won't know it 'cause he only goes to his earmarked pages. When he wakes he won't be missin' somethin' he doesn't know he had. *(Beat)* And I need it to wipe 'cause he won't let me use the party newspaper. *(She puts the torn pages in her pocket, then stands over her father.)* I'm goin' to bed. You still asleep? *(She lightly brushes his hair once, but doesn't want to wake him.)* Still a handsome man. But I can't remember her like you do 'cause I was only six but she must of loved you up 'til you couldn't stand it anymore. Because you never seemed to need to find it again. What was it like, Daddy, to be loved like that?

I lied to you. My husband's eyes are not open in his grave. They were closed when he lived and closed when he died. He never could bear to look at me. I mean, really look at me. You ever have a hand touch you like it was touchin' a table, or reachin' for a bowl of soup? Then you'd know me.

On Sacred Ground
by Susan Rowan Masters

In this poignant original monologue, Onatah, an eloquent and sensitive Native American teenager, sits in an empty bedroom on a Seneca reservation in western New York State mourning the loss of her home and the changes that are being thrust upon her and the other native families in town. Using her grandfather's Talking Stick, Onatah paints an emotional portrait of how she came to an understanding — and even a kind of acceptance — of the changes she and other Seneca families are facing as they try to transform pained resignation into a cautious and hopeful optimism for justice.

ONATAH: *(Enters holding a canvas bag.)* This is my bedroom. It's empty now like all the other rooms in all the other houses here. Grandfather drove me an' him back for one last visit before they burn everything. They destroy our houses and give us new ones we never wanted in the first place. Just so they can take our ... *(Pause)* But I'm getting ahead of myself. *(She opens the bag and takes out a Talking Stick.)* Grandfather made this Talking Stick. You see, how it works is the person holding it can speak their truth. The others have to listen until it's their turn to hold it.

Anyway, Grandfather made it special out of birch for that meeting he and the other tribal elders had with the government men. *(She sits down cross-legged on the floor and cradles the Talking Stick in her hands.)* That was two years ago. Back when the elders and my parents started talking in whispers around us kids. I was eleven then and old enough to know something was up. Besides, I'd heard things at school. So when Grandfather went to that meeting, well, I was determined to find out. I planned to hang around the house so I'd be there when he returned. I got out my school books and sat by the window pretending to do homework. That kept Mother from putting me to work in the kitchen. Every five minutes I'd glance out the window hoping to see him. Just when I was beginning to think he'd show up after Mother had sent me to bed, I saw him in the distance.

I ran to the door, but Mother called me back. "Don't burden your Grandfather, Onatah," she said. I wanted to shout, "Burden *him?* What about me?" But Mother was already in a poor mood, so I said nothing and went back to my school books. When Grandfather came in I noticed how stooped he walked, as if carrying the whole Seneca Nation on his shoulders. He didn't speak but went over to his chair and placed the Walking Stick into his bag beside the chair. I waited till Mother left the room before asking the question that had been boiling up in me. "Some of the older kids are saying everyone has to leave here. Is it true, Grandfather?" He just sat there with his head cradled in his hands. "I *deserve* to know," I told him. Finally he got up. "Get your coat," he said. I grabbed it and followed him into the cool night.

We walked to the edge of town past the Longhouse. Then Grandfather led me over our forefathers' sacred ground and up a hillside where he stopped at the crest. Below, the Allegheny River shimmered in the moonlight. He just stood there, silent. I tugged on his jacket sleeve, calling his name. Finally he spoke the words I will always carry with me. "Look around, Granddaughter," he said, stretching out his arms. "Soon all this will be under water. Government men call the dam 'progress.' They break our treaty and force us from the land of our ancestors." I clamped my hands over my ears. *"No,"* I cried. *"We won't go."* Grandfather reached for me, but I turned away. Oh, I didn't mean to disrespect him like that. Regret pulled me back around. Grandfather was picking a blade of grass. He straightened to his full six feet and held the blade up where it caught a breeze. "See how this is forced to bend for a time, Onatah?" he said. "But the wind can *never* break its spirit." *(Long pause)* I think I heard Grandfather calling. I have to go now. *(She stands up and slowly looks around, observing the empty room, then faces the audience.)* No matter what happens, I'm going to be OK. *(She puts the Talking Stick into the bag.)* I just know I am. *(She squares her shoulders and exits.)*

Pretty Theft
by Adam Szymkowicz

Allegra is a lively and emotionally complex teenager, estranged at times from her parents and wrestling with the lingering trauma of her father's death following a prolonged stay in the hospital while in a coma. Although she struggles to regain her bearings after the loss of her father, she also resolves to become more assertive and independent. Here, Allegra takes the first step and informs her mother that instead of going to the funeral, she's taking off on a cross-country trip with her friend, Suzy.

ALLEGRA: I know you're probably mad at me for leaving before the funeral, but I just can't do it. My whole body itches and it won't stop until I get in a car and can't see this house or this town or this state from the rearview window. This way is better. This way I'll come back from my trip and go straight to school and you won't have to look at me or think about me. You can tell people you have a daughter, but you won't have to talk to me on the phone or see me on the couch. I'll be a no-maintenance daughter just like you always wanted. I'm going to go now. I know someday you'll want to talk to me again. Maybe after I graduate and get a job and get married and buy a house and have my own daughter. Then you can talk to her and be her favorite, and then we can pretend you were a really great mother. She won't know, and I don't have to tell her.

But now I'm going to get on the road and push you out of my mind, and I probably won't think of you until I get to the Grand Canyon or some other fairly good canyon. And maybe I'll cry in front of the mammoth orange hole in the ground, or maybe I'll smile because it's so beautiful and I'm free and windswept. But first I'm going to get into Suzy's mom's car and we'll drive till there's just drops left in the tank and as we cross the border into Massachusetts, we'll roll into the first gas station where I'll get some Ding Dongs and some orange soda and I'll bite into the first one sitting on the hood, watching the car slurp up gas. Then I'll get in the driver's seat and put my foot on the accelerator until I can't keep my eyes open anymore. So I pull over and we both close our eyes and sleep until we're awoken at three a.m. by separate but equally terrible nightmares.

Veils

by Tom Coash

In this original monologue, Intisar, a devout, strong-willed and passionate young African American Muslim, stands poised on a bare stage wearing a hijab (veil) to voice her belief that charity and understanding are more than a match for either duplicity or unfeeling prejudice. Her personal story of the September 11, 2001 tragedy is a heartfelt examination of the emergence of a "new world" as well as an elegy for a certain time and place in America that was shattered that day in New York City. Intisar shares her views on the strange turn of events that transformed a very fragile beginning into a more authentic life in spite of the disquieting truths that have emerged since then.

INTISAR: 9/11, 2001, right? My mother ... was forced to strip to her underwear in the back room of an airport. I was thirteen and we were flying home from my aunt's wedding. Halfway there our plane was diverted to a small airport. Nobody knew what was happening. We didn't know of the hijackings or that all flights were being grounded. We were on the runway for more than an hour when airport security came on the plane. Searching, apparently, for anybody who looked dangerous and proceeded to escort my mother and me onto the tarmac, everybody staring. In a back room full of security, they had our suitcases open, belongings strewn all over, and my mother was requested to submit to a body search. When she refused, the requests became uglier, strip or be arrested. She looked at me, afraid, tears running down my face, and she took her clothes off. Of course they found nothing. What was there to find? They looked at me and she said, "You will *not* undress my daughter." They didn't but they made me take my veil off. Why is that? What did they think I might be hiding under a dang scarf?

It was my first veil. When a girl reaches puberty. I hadn't even had it a month. Delicate, light blue. Like the sky we had been flying through. A proud moment. Becoming a woman. A rite of passage. I hadn't had it a month and a person of supposed authority forced me to take it off. Raghead.

Later, I sat crying next to my mother as we waited for my father to drive four hundred miles to rescue us. She asked why I was crying and I said, "Shame." My mother replied, "Daughter, another person cannot inflict shame on you. Only you can inflict shame on yourself. When those men looked at my body, my naked skin, they were the ones who felt shame. Because God was not in their hearts. Keep God strong in your heart and you will never feel shame."

They kept asking my mother where we were from. Like we weren't American. Like we were foreigners. She would say, "Overbrook Park." "Where is that?" "Philadelphia," she would say. And they would look at her like she was making a joke. What was she supposed to say? Africa? Fula? Futa Toro? Where my great, great, *great* grandmother was stolen out of her bed, raped and dragged to America in chains? And the first thing they did, when she got to the Land of the Free, was strip her naked and put her on the auction block ... She wasn't hiding anything either.

I want to answer a few questions about this, my veil, my hijab. No, it is not hot. No, my father doesn't make me wear it. And no, I am not oppressed. No need to call Oprah. The right to wear clothes, to cover yourself, is important to my family. This veil connects me to my God, to my family and to our history of struggle. When I put on this veil, I know who I am. There is a simplicity. A clarity. I know who I am and who I want to be. This veil is not hiding away. For me, it is a release. Without it I feel naked. I am naked.

"Tell the believing women to lower their gaze and be modest, and to display of their adornment only that which is apparent, and to draw their veils over their bosoms." That seems pretty clear to me. God says wear a veil, you do it, right? I believe in this. I am strong in my heart. I'm not hiding anything.

(Costume Note: The "hijab" is wrapped snugly around the head covering the hair but not the face. Looking online you will find a variety of veil styles and specific instructions on how to put them on correctly.)

The Clean House
by Sarah Ruhl

In this 2005 Pulitzer Prize finalist play, Matilde, a whimsical Brazilian woman with a delightfully unorthodox sense of humor, is in America working as a cleaning lady for a wealthy couple. Her mission, however, is to honor her parents — "the funniest people in Brazil" — by composing the perfect joke. In this somber and chilling direct address to the audience, Matilde talks about how her parents died as the result of a series of comic mishaps and tragic wisecracks. There is a generous slice of dark irony and a hefty dose of wicked humor in Matilde's monologue that underscores human misery but also reveals bittersweet truths about sad and funny incidents that are the very stuff of life.

MATILDE: The story of my parents is this. It was said that my father was the funniest man in his village. He did not marry until he was sixty-three because he did not want to marry a woman who was not funny. He said he would wait until he met his match in wit.

And then one day he met my mother. He used to say: Your mother — and he would take a long pause — *(MATILDE takes a long pause)* is funnier than I am. We have never been apart since the day we met, because I always wanted to know the next joke.

My mother and father did not look into each other's eyes. They laughed like hyenas. Even when they made love they laughed like hyenas. My mother was old for a mother. She refused many proposals. It would kill her, she said, to have to spend her days laughing at jokes that were not funny. *(Pause)*

I wear black because I am in mourning. My mother died last year. Have you ever heard the expression, "I almost died laughing"? Well that's what she did. The doctors couldn't explain it. They argued, they said she choked on her own spit, but they don't really know. She was laughing at one of my father's jokes. A joke he took one year to make up, for the anniversary of their marriage. When my mother died laughing, my father shot himself. And so I came here, to clean this house.

Shawna

by Sofia Dubrawsky

In this original dramatic monologue, Shawna, a strong-willed, independent fourteen-year-old girl, is battling the ravages of cancer and the implications that could change her life forever. Here, she is at a recreational summer camp designed for teens in treatment and is performing a personal ceremony on the beach at night as part of a "sharing" exercise by each of the camp participants. Standing in a circle with her cabin mates, Shawna holds a stick, a rock, and a shell in her hands as she voices a heartrending narrative that leaves us with a lingering note of hope and faith that the scars of her battle will not be long in healing.

SHAWNA: This stick represents cancer ... I'm ready to let it go forever ... *(She throws the stick into the ocean.)*
This rock represents my fear, the nightmare I keep having. It's, I'm — I'm lying on this big table, but actually it isn't a table, it's more like a hospital bed maybe, I'm not sure but I can't move and it's really cold. Everyone is around me: my mom, my sister, Dr. Kelston and the nurses. And they are all staring down at me, smiling, laughing, and they are talking to each other, like they're having a party. And they are eating something weird, pink and red. They are stuffing their mouths and their cheeks are all greasy, and they're licking their lips and fingers like it's chicken but it's not. I try to talk to them, but they don't hear me. And then I look down and see there is a hole in my belly and they are reaching in with their hands and pulling out pieces of my body and eating me! Scooping their hands in and pulling out parts of me! I start screaming, "Stop! Stop it!" but they don't stop, they don't even hear me. Then I look down further and see my legs are gone. I just have these two stumps left. Then my mom suddenly barges forward, she grabs the biggest handful of all and laughs really loud. I see my insides all around, chunks of pink, red meat and organs falling everywhere, and people are just smacking their mouths and teeth, grinning down at me! I look down again and the hole looks empty. I'm almost gone! I force myself to wake up. This rock is that dream, and I never want to have it

again! *(She throws the rock as far as she can.)*

And this shell represents the new friends that I made this summer. I picked the shell for my friends because it's beautiful. I found it down there near the driftwood, and I'm going to keep it with me forever. Yes, forever.

Random Women
by Carolyn Carpenter

Rosalia, a kind and good-natured Hispanic woman with a sometimes irreverent sense of humor, is as amusing as she is compassionate and thought-provoking in this original monologue that illuminates with graceful prose the deep recesses of sadness that lie just beneath the surface of her job as a caregiver for children of working parents. Her story examines the behind-the-scenes intrigues and struggles that are part of being a Hispanic woman in America without a green card and the limited options available to those struggling to be part of the "American Dream." What surfaces, however, is the poignant portrait of a warmhearted woman who has discovered the love of children — even though they are not hers — is the best reward that life has to offer.

ROSALIA: I love children. I'm good with them. Because I haven't forgotten what it is to be a child. It's so fresh in my memory that sometimes it surprises me when I'm treated like an adult. Children bring such life into the world. Energy. And I appreciate them for that gift. Maybe it's because I can't have children of my own. And in my family … well, that's not a good thing. I can't adopt. Coming here has ruined my chances to ever raise children of my own. So, I raise other people's kids.

I have worked for seven families in ten years. So far, I have nurtured fifteen children through their first six years of life. I'm hired by working parents, single parents, overwrought parents, and lazy parents. Often I pick up the babies at five in the morning and don't return them until seven at night. Five, sometimes six, days a week. Usually the babies come to me at about five months, although I've had as young as seven weeks. And when the kids start school, sometimes I'm let go. Boarding school, private classes, public education ... these are the new parents. And I never see my babies again. All I can do is pray that I touched their lives. At least I know they'll be bilingual. *(Laughs.)* Oh, I make the parents so mad. "Please speak English to my child," they tell me. I nod and smile. Then I forget. OK, maybe I don't forget. Maybe I decide bilingual is better. Maybe I want to expand the child's mind. Maybe I want to help the babies learn not to separate themselves through language, or religion, or color. I suppose the parents don't like it because the children often spend so much time with me, they can't speak English. So it becomes my fault the parents can't communicate with their own children. Then they fire me. Oh, they make a big production out of it too. So the babies can see how mommy or daddy is protecting them from the evil language. It's OK that I change diapers and give baths and monitor fevers ... but communicate?

Who do I think I am? You know, I'm not stupid. I know these parents hire me because I'm cheap labor. Because they can cheat me and there is no one I can turn to. Because I'm helpless without a green card. But I don't understand why I mean nothing in a society that trusts me with its children. With its future. What these two-car, new-house, career-minded, American-dream parents fail to realize is that ... from a child's perspective ... they are the aliens. *(Pause)* Often my final words to my babies ... their babies ... are, "Te amo, los niños. Don't forget your Spanish, and you won't forget me." Then I turn and leave as quickly as possible. Humming to drown out their familiar cries. *(She looks at the baby, smiles gently, and returns to singing.)*

CHAPTER 5
A TIME OF DOUBT

"If you would be a real seeker after truth,
it is necessary that at least once in your life you doubt."
— Rene Descartes, *Passions of the Soul*

There is a touch of bittersweet melancholy and regret in the characters that find themselves in a time of doubt at isolated periods in their lives. Plunged into complex and complicated situations or relationships, the characters' soul-searching and heart-wrenching observations are sometimes absurd, sometimes puzzling, but always compassionate. Although the characters in this chapter may gain new perspectives or cultivate new values, there is also an emotional price to be paid for their relationships that dissolve or unravel with unexpected results.

The authors cast a spell of charm and menace at the same time, and their character choices will keep you guessing in each monologue. These riveting portraits offer truthful points of view with charm, sharp wit, and a surge of emotional ferocity that, while disturbing at times, is entirely relevant and unique to communicate each character's time of doubt. The authors' acute observations also make for a good thriller in some instances and some surprising twists in other instances.

In spite of a number of fractured fairy tale endings, this collection showcases a gallery of vibrant character portraits. There are funny, sad, and profane characters all skillfully wrapped up in a neat package waiting for their theatrical moment. You will find it very difficult not to be part of this tender and honest celebration of each character's time of doubt.

Miss Witherspoon

by Christopher Durang

Veronica Witherspoon, an eccentric and offbeat woman with a sardonic sense of humor, finds the world a frightening place ever since Skylab — the unmanned American space station — came crashing down to Earth. Disillusioned and delirious with fear and her stifling life, Veronica committed suicide and now finds herself in what she expected to be heaven but is instead something call the Bardo ("Netherworld" in Tibetian Buddhism). Although the spiritual forces there keep trying to help her reincarnate, Veronica's "spiritual otherworldly emergency brake system" always seems to fail and she finds herself returned to earth … where, each time, she keeps killing herself.

VERONICA: Well, I'm dead. I committed suicide in the 1990s because of Skylab. Well, not entirely, but it's as sensible an explanation as anything. Most of you don't remember what Skylab was … I seem to have had a disproportionate reaction to it, most people seemed to have sluffed it off. Skylab was this American space station, it was thousands of tons of heavy metal, and it got put up into orbit over the Earth sometime in the '70s.

Eventually the people onboard abandoned it, and it was just floating up there; and you'd think the people who put it up there would have had a plan for how to get it back to Earth again, but they didn't. Or the plan failed, or something; and in 1979 they announced that Skylab would eventually be falling from the sky in a little bit — this massive thing the size of a city block might come crashing down on your head as you stood in line at Bloomingdale's or sat by your suburban pool, or as you were crossing the George Washington Bridge, et cetera, et cetera.

Of course, *statistically,* the likelihood of Skylab hitting you on the head — or rather hitting the whole bunch of you on the head — statistically the odds were small. But I can't live my life by statistics. And the experts didn't think it through, I guess. Sure, let's put massive tonnage up in the sky. I'm sure it won't fall down. Sure, let's build nuclear power plants. I'm sure we'll figure out what to do with radioactive waste *eventually.*

Well, you can start to see I have the kind of personality that might kill myself. I mean, throw in unhappy relationships and a kind of dark, depressive tinge to my psychology, and something like Skylab just sends me over the edge. *"I can't live in a world where there is Skylab!"* — I sort of screamed this out in the airport as I was in some endless line waiting to go away to somewhere or other.

So I died sometime in the '90s. Obviously it was a *delayed* reaction to Skylab. So I killed myself. Anger turned inward, they say. But at least I got to miss 9/11. If I couldn't stand Skylab, I definitely couldn't stand the sight of people jumping out of windows. And then letters with anthrax postmarked from Trenton, New Jersey. And in some quarters people danced in the streets in celebration. "Oh, lots of people killed, yippee, yippee, yippee." God, I hate human beings. I'm glad I killed myself.

You know, in the afterlife I'm considered to have a bad attitude.

Bums

by Robert Shaffron

Evelyn, an emotionally fragile teenage girl, is a present day nomad — one of the familiar "street people" of society forced to face the bittersweet consequences of choices made long ago in haste. Her struggle to survive the emotional hurricane that has ripped through her young life resonates with an honesty and simplicity that sharply underlines a sense of guilt and remorse that lies just beneath the surface. In rekindling memories of her childhood, Evelyn remains shackled by her past and unable to embrace a hopeful future.

EVELYN: I don't know when I stopped living my life and my life started living me. (Beat) My mother was a Christian. A Bible-slamming, fire-and-brimstone, hallelujah Christian. I remember the day — the night — of her conversion. I was sleeping. She tore into the apartment — I slept on the couch — and she was out of breath, and her hair was, well, some of it had slipped out from under the elastic band she always had it pulled back in. And she ran around the room turning on all the lamps, and she turned on the light in the little half-kitchen, and she turned on the lights in her bedroom and left the door open so the light came into the living room where I was sleeping.

I sat up. I was scratching and trying to straighten the crumpled sheets under me. With my eyes closed the lights were so bright and I asked her, "Ma, why are you turning all the lights on like that? It hurts my eyes." And she rushed over to me and she pulled me off the couch onto the floor and said, "Evelyn, we're gonna get down on our knees and pray. In the light. And we're gonna pray to the Lord that we may always live in the light. The clean, pure holy light that falls down on us from the good Lord in heaven."

We'd never prayed in our lives. I didn't even know what praying was, really. I knew people prayed in church. I'd seen pictures of churches, and they always looked beautiful and scary with the colored lights all coming through the stained glass windows and shiny wood benches and gigantic stone arches and I wondered how we were gonna pray in our little apartment with the greasy walls and the chipped tile floors and bare light bulbs — scary but not beautiful like the churches. *(Beat)*

All mother wanted was a man who wouldn't leave her, so she brought God home. And he stayed. Mother went crazy with religion. As soon as I was old enough, I did the only thing I could think to do. I got pregnant and left home. Amen.

Daughter
by Elana Gartner

In this engrossing original monologue, Millie, an adventurous and free-spirited biker chick who masks her charm and compassion with a hard and gruff exterior, has just met Robyn — the biological daughter she gave up sixteen years ago. The two women gradually warm to each other and Millie shares the sad story of Robyn's father, a young boy with whom she had fallen in love and who was killed in a tragic accident without so much as a farewell good-bye. Burdened by his death and the bitterness of the past, Millie also confesses that she has always regretted giving her daughter up for adoption.

MILLIE: Right. Boyfriends. Right. So one night, at the campground, this guy comes through. And he's really wild. And he just had this energy — you just wanted to be with him all the time, you know? And, out of everyone there, he wanted to be with me. He stayed at Blackbird Perch for a good week or so. And I stayed with him every single night. And he was a fantastic lover. *(Beat)*

That's probably not the stuff I should be telling you about your dad. You probably don't want to be hearing that kind of stuff. Anyhow, he was wild and dreamy. I really thought this was it. I thought, "Wow. This is it. This is what it's really like to be in love." Or whatever that means. At sixteen, can you imagine? And, there he was, just talking to me, spending every waking minute with me, looking up at the stars with me every night. It was like a dream. Really, I thought I'd died right there and gone to heaven. But … *(Beat)*

One morning he was out in the woods, looking for some berries or something. And, you know, he must have lost track of where he was and wandered way off into another part of the forest where people are really not supposed to go. I mean, he had a pretty good sense of direction so you had to think he knew something, but he wandered right into the hunting area. And, you know what? *(She puts a finger to her head like a gun and makes gunshot noise.)* Just like that. Really quick, too. The hunter found him immediately and tried to get help, but it was too late. A friend of my uncle's, actually. They used to hunt together all the time. He just felt terrible. Never forgave himself. Even stopped hunting for a while. And, after his funeral, that's when I found out. I was pregnant with … *(Beat)* I wanted to keep you, but my mom wouldn't let me. She said that the baby was going to bring bad spirits on the family.

She even closed Blackbird Perch after that. Sold it. She said it had bad juju. I never really believed that kind of stuff. But she marched me right to the clinic and signed me up to have you adopted. I never even got to hold you in the hospital. They took you right away. But I was always mad about it. So, when mom died last year, I made up my mind to try to find you.

Look What You Made Me Do
by Lynda Sturner

Grace, a mysterious, well-groomed, and well-dressed woman with a deeply affecting gaze, stands awkwardly in front of a circle of other women at the local shelter holding a small hand-sized memo machine called a VOICE IT. There is a veneer of subtle but ominous uncertainty about her, and she speaks at an alarming rate as the suspense builds layer upon layer toward a gripping climax. While Grace's mood at first is lighthearted and punctuated with brightly humorous lines, secrets that were largely unspoken suddenly burst forth, and we realize that Grace is not what she appears to be or what we expect.

GRACE: I don't belong here, really. I thought I could just sit in and, you know, listen. But OK if we all have to take a turn … I can do that … sure. Guess you don't usually see people like me in places like this. I'm probably wasting everybody's time. Oh, it's wonderful what you do here … taking women in … hiding them and all … terrific service … safe and … excuse me a minute, please.

(GRACE takes out a small memo machine — VOICE IT — and turns it on. It beeps.) Asparagus, sweet potatoes. *(GRACE releases button.)* My shopping list. *(GRACE remembers where she is.)*

Safe. You're Angela, right? And you're Kisha and Robin, no, no Robby. So I remember your names. I heard you speak at the benefit luncheon at the Marriott Hotel last month … where Elizabeth Taylor was supposed to moderate but … well I forget the reason … anyway Rosie filled in … She's funny … but I mean when you pay two hundred dollars and you're seated at the back of the room behind 1200 women … but I didn't come here to complain that they served fish … or that you couldn't even get a second glass of wine … not that the first one was that great but you know wine is wine is … wine.

(GRACE presses memo machine.) Cauliflower. *(GRACE releases button.)*

I should go home. I can't stop thinking about your stories. Oh, God. I'm doing just what Brian hates. Does this drive you crazy too … that I never finish a thought? He says listening to me is like Chinese water torture. But I finish thoughts all the time … in my head. I start to say something to him, and then I see this trapped look on his face … so I forget what I started to say and talk about vegetables. Vegetables are always safe. I'll say, for instance … the Supreme Court made a big mistake, and I think, ahhhh … are those mushrooms done the way you like them, dear? Not enough garlic. Oh, I'm sorry. But I say lots of interesting things when he's not around. I do. When I'm alone thoughts flow, I'm clear, precise. I talk to this machine. I tell it things. If there's an editorial I disagree with or a conversation I wish I had, I just push the button and off I go and when I listen back, I even like myself sometimes.

(GRACE holds up the machine.) This is my new machine. *(GRACE touches the machine lovingly and protectively and switches it on.)* Broccoli, celery, brussels sprouts. *(Releases button.)* I should go. *(GRACE caresses the machine.)* Look, it's not as if he beats me. He doesn't do that. Brian's a screamer. Does that count? And he throws things, but at the walls, not at me. I mean, I understand when I've been wrong, like when I forget to fill the car up with gas or don't put rice in the salt shaker and it doesn't pour, but sometimes he's angry and I don't know what I've done. Like that night we were having breast of chicken with orange glaze … he's muttering under his breath, "stupid cow" and throws his plate against the wall. I had made him fruit cup and some of the glass from the salad bowl which he threw landed in the fruit, then he freaked 'cause there was no dessert. Look what you made me do, he says. He's broken all of my grandmother's dishes. I can't talk about these things with my friends. But it's not as if he hits me.

(GRACE turns on the machine.) Carrots, peas, artichokes … shhhh … shhhh … shhhh. *(GRACE turns off the machine.)* I keep thinking about your story, Angela. How it started out as a game with your husband. You were the puppy and he was the master, and then he kept … wouldn't let you out of the cage, and now you're into hiking and for the first time in your life, every step you take belongs to you. Every step you take belongs … All of your stories … when I heard them, it was like when I first saw *Rent,* that musical, I wanted to jump on stage and be them. *(Sings "La Vie Boheme.")*

(GRACE turns on the machine.) I killed Brian with my veggie prep knife this morning. *(GRACE turns off the machine.)* Just kidding.

(Laughs.) Oh God, that felt good. Can I say it again? *(GRACE turns on the machine.)* I killed Brian. *(Laughs.)* Brian's dead ... dead dead dead dead dead dead dead. *(GRACE replays dead dead dead dead dead dead dead while she talks.)* He broke my memo machine. All I did was ask him to listen to it. Let me talk when I wasn't afraid to finish a sentence. Please, I said to Brian, just listen, but he took it and smashed it into the side of the kitchen counter. *(GRACE holds up the machine.)* This is my new one. Bought it today before I came here. My new machine. *(GRACE holds the machine to her heart.)* I'm not going home. 'Cause it wasn't like I'd forgotten to fill the car with gas or overcooked the pasta or run out of orange juice ... can I stay here?

A Confluence of Dreaming
by Tammy Ryan

Carol, an exasperated, suburban, stay-at-home mother, has discovered that her teenage daughter, Morgan, has been having a "cyber affair" with a stranger she met on the Internet and is overwhelmed with bewilderment and frustration. The tenuous mother/daughter relationship is already emotionally complex, and what follows is a heated argument about whether or not her daughter is going to college. But, in this exchange, Carol also reveals a cynical sense of her own delusion about romantic love and perhaps her own marriage.

CAROL: Every generation thinks it's going to change the world, you are not the first, but you'll grow up and you'll see it can't be done. The only thing you can do is take care of yourself, and that's what I'm trying to help you do. Go to college, get an education, get a job. Then you can do what you want — but I see already what's going to happen to you. 'Cause you won't think any more than I did. You'll meet some guy, fall in love, and get married. And then everything you want now will go out the window. Because you'll have kids and you won't have time for any of this nonsense anymore. Because you'll be just like me, Morgan, living day to day: going shopping, cooking meals, yes, cleaning the house, doing the laundry, taking the cat to the vet, taking care of everyone else, and there won't be time for any other nonsense, like worrying about who we're bombing. Because we are always bombing someone! And what you have to do today nibbles and nibbles and nibbles away until there's nothing left. Your concept of the planet will shrink to the size of your kitchen island and humanity will be the people sitting around it who have hooked up their vacuum cleaners to your jugular and have sucked, sucked, sucked everything out until your soul has become as dry as a desert. *(CAROL bursts into tears.)*

So don't talk to me about my soul.

Cold-Blooded Murderer
by Elisa Thompson

This chilling and sinister original monologue is an intriguing game of cat and mouse played by Elizabeth — a callous and cynical young girl who has just confessed to murdering six other girls — and the police officers who are interrogating her. Elizabeth's confession strips away layers of psychological secrets and ugly truths that paint a compelling portrait of a young girl whose life has been rife with recrimination and the need to be recognized. The sense of horror and outrage depicted here will challenge the heart and mind in its moral complexity and no doubt linger on in your memory without providing easy answers.

ELIZABETH: You want to know, I suppose, what turns a nice little girl like me into a cold-blooded murderer. You want the truth? You want to know why I did it? Why I killed all those girls? It's because I like it. I don't expect you to understand what it's like. You have no idea. To hold someone's life in your hands. To be in control.

There's always that moment of acknowledgement between a killer and their victim. That instant when she realizes your power, and she looks at you and you look at her, and she pleads with her eyes. She begs for mercy, for her life. And you have a split second to decide: to save her, well that's great. You could give her life back, give her back to her family and friends, the people that love her. But to kill her … That's something different. To remove her from this earth, to take away the thing that most value above all: her life. Now that's real power. None of these girls deserved their lives. Look at them! The musician, the actor, the writer, the dancer, the artist, the model. None of them appreciated what they had. They were the best. And that meant nothing to them. I've never been the best. Always smart, but never the smartest. Pretty, but never the prettiest. Talented, but never the most talented. But despite all this, I always thought I was special. I thought there was something inside me, lurking within, that would make me great. I've never been content with the idea of simply living my life, dying, and being forgotten. That's just not me. I want to be remembered for my achievements. And I will be, won't I? Sure, you're disgusted by what I've done. You're horrified. You think I'm a monster. But I can guarantee that you're not going to go home to your boring lives and just forget me. Oh, no. I'm willing to bet I'll be on your mind for quite some time.

I used to think I could find other ways to be recognized. I wanted to be famous for a while. But then I realized how stupid that is. People would want to be me, without really knowing what that means. Then I thought of being a lawyer ... Me! I thought, "If I save lives, people will worship me." But I realized, not long ago now, not long before I killed for the first time, that saving people isn't enough. I could save the lives of one hundred people, and they would be grateful, and so would their families and friends. But what about everyone else? They'd see me on the news and think, "Huh. That's nice." Then change the channel to something else. But what if I killed just one person, and not just kill them, but brutally murder them. With my bare hands, staring them right in the eye. Not for revenge, not for personal gain, but because I like killing. People would pay attention then. The whole world would stop, with me in the center. Everyone looking at me.

And I know what you're all thinking. I can see the looks in your faces. You think I'm just an attention-seeking little kid, but I'm not. I just want someone to notice me. All my life I've stayed in the background. There's always been that one student who gets better marks than me. That one teacher who makes me feel stupid, that one friend who always shuts me down, that one parent who's not interested, that one sibling who overshadows my achievements with theirs. And nobody even cares. I just want you to think. And don't act like this doesn't apply to you, Sergeant, 'cause it does. You're just the sort to do it. You've done it to me … Next time you're going to put someone down, point out their faults, make them feel stupid, belittle them, think about me, then think about them, and what they could do to you. How much would you respect them if they had their hands around your neck, and they had the choice: to release their grip on your throat, or to just keep pressing. Think about it.

In the Daylight
by Tony Glazer

Jessie, the youngest and most vulnerable sibling in the dysfunctional Feingold family, offers a vivid and riveting account of the real reason her brother, Martin, has been summoned home so urgently. She is feisty, combative, and unsentimental as she unravels the horrific story of her father's plan to kill all of the family and then take his own life. With cruel precision, Jessie mocks her brother and questions his family loyalty as we witness the sobering truth that she has a cold, murderous side to her personality.

JESSIE: Do you really want to know about that night, Martin? Do you really want all the details? You can't even go upstairs to the bedroom where it happened. How are you going to be able to absorb how I cut that man up? That's right. Mom fell apart. You ran away. I was the only one left. You thought *she* did everything? That's just what we told you. You already hated her for sleeping with another man. If you hated me too, we'd never get you back here, and getting you back was key. Everything we did was specifically crafted for maximum manipulation. All avenues explored in order to get you back and soften you up once here. Right down to Mom's "oh so mortal" phone call and my "oh so serious" health update. You want to talk about that night? Good. Let's talk about it. Our father was going to kill us all and then kill himself, but he dropped dead before he could do it. Yet while this family suddenly had a second chance, there was still a man shot to death in the bedroom. No matter what story we came up with, we would have never survived the scandal. Dad's legacy, this family's legacy, was in jeopardy. Someone had to do something, so I did it. It was it was ugly. But it had to happen. So tell me, Martin. Now that your courage up, what else would you like to know about that night? Do you want to know what tools I used? Which ones were great for flesh? Which ones for hacking through bone? Do you want to hear all the trial and error with cutting tools? Why a chain saw, despite popular movie wisdom, is the worst thing to use? Would you like to know how messy it gets with a chain saw? No? How about which corrosive solvents Dad had downstairs that eat flesh and organs without cutting or burning? Products you can buy at any hardware store. How about the bones, Martin? Would you like to hear how, with a hammer, I broke up the bones into little bitty bite-size pieces before systematically burning them all to ashes in Dad's incinerator? Do you want me to itemize the carnage of that night, because I will if it will make you face your own complicity in it. It's truth time, Martin. None of us can move forward until you decide once and for all where you stand. You're going to have to admit to me, admit to us, that you're a part of this family, because without family everything else is a lie. What's it going to be, big brother? Yes or no. In or out.

All Aboard the Marriage Hearse
by Matt Morillo

Amy, a mature and self-confident young woman with courage and spirit, has just ended her long-term relationship with live-in boyfriend Sean because he refuses to get married. This compelling personal portrait of a young woman experiencing first love and then suddenly bursting into adulthood with all its struggles and disappointments offers candid insight into Amy's realization of the sobering truth that there is more that divides her relationship with Sean than unites them.

AMY: All my life, I believed in the fairy tale of "the one." Every guy I've ever dated I wondered, "Is it him?" And I made myself sick over it and I probably drove every one of those guys crazy … Let me finish. But it wasn't until last night that I realized how cynical that idea is. How cynical is it to suggest that in a world of six billion people,

113

there is only one person that can make you happy? How silly is that? And how crazy do we all make ourselves wondering about that? How much extra unnecessary pressure does that put on relationships? Then we feel this inclination to commit our entire lives to this person because we foolishly believe that they are the only one that could ever make us happy. Well, I'm no longer going to be a slave to that train of thought. So with the next guy I date, I won't put that pressure on him or myself. I'll just live day by day and whatever happens, happens. Perhaps there is no such thing as "the one." Just the one right now.

We were each the one for the past two years and nine months, until last night. But stop interrupting me, because I'm trying to thank you. Thanks to you, this breakup is going to be much easier to take for me. I won't get absorbed in the drama of it all. I'll do my crying, and move on to the next guy. Now please give me my phone.

When It's Over
by Christyna Belden

In this original monologue, a young Nameless Woman enters cradling a worn, tattered jacket and slowly moves Center Stage. She turns to the audience, looking torn and abused, and we sense unanswered questions seeking answers, disturbing truths to be revealed, and a single-mindedness of purpose to exorcise ghosts of the recent past in order to deal with the present and the future. Partly speaking to the audience, partly speaking to herself, and partly glancing up toward the heavens, the Nameless Woman shares a sobering tale of sorrow and shattered hopes after making a fateful decision rather than face ridicule and scorn.

NAMELESS WOMAN: He said it would be easy, that no one would know. Just go quietly and have it done, after all, he said, it is only a little procedure. He said it was my responsibility to handle it, that I should have been more careful in the first place. I asked him to not make me go alone … He said he would call me later when it was done.

And so I went, alone and scared … not sure what I was doing or why. It had to be the only choice, the right thing to do … didn't it? I mean, after all, I'm young and I have my whole life in front of me. It was just one little mistake; I can't let that ruin my life ... or his.

One of the other girls there began to talk to me. Her name was Jenny. She was chewing gum nonchalantly and just chatting away. She said this was her second time and that it wasn't a big deal anymore. Her eyes looked hard and hollow, but I just figured that was the type of person she was.

They called my name and in I went. It didn't take long really ... just signing some papers, lying on the cold table, and then before I knew it ... it was over ... and they were right. It really was a simple little process, done quickly and efficiently ... afterwards whooshing you out the door so they can get on to the next in line.

That was days ago ... I still haven't been home. Did he call that night? I don't really know. Would I have spoken to him? I can't really say. But they forget something. They don't tell you about the ache. Not a pain in your body, but a pain that goes deep into your heart and feels like it will never go away. That is why I can't go home. My family will see it on me, the pain that is ... I know I won't be able to hide it. Now I understood why Jenny looked like she did. This makes you hard and hollow.

Why didn't they tell me about this part? Where you want to die inside, where you wonder if it really was the only choice. Did I really have to? Was it really my only option? Will God ever forgive me? Will I ever forgive myself? *(Collapses on the stage cradling the bundle.)* I think I would have named her Emily.

Barrio Hollywood
by Elaine Romero

Graciela, a fiery and headstrong Latina ballet folklorico dancer, is being interrogated by the local police to discover what she knows about the possible murder of her brother, Alex. The younger brother received a traumatic blow to the head while boxing and, although not expected to recover, quite suddenly died. The police suspect that Ama, his mother, may have "mercy killed" him. During the interrogation, the suspense quickly becomes twisted in a real-life game of cat and mouse as Graciela's sense of truth and illusion become almost inseparably entangled.

GRACIELA: We all wanted to believe. See, where I come from, if you have faith, God has pity on you and makes things better. It's like He reaches His hand into your head and captures whatever picture you hold there. And if you imagine it just right, He'll set his hand down on earth and set that picture free. He makes it real. But you've got to believe. That's the first rule of faith. I told my mother we could imagine Alex healthy. Just like she taught me. We would create this powerful image of him. I could see him right there. So beautiful. *(Beat)* I don't know where it went. Has that ever happened to you? Someone you love dies and you just can't see them anymore? *(Beat)* My mother? She does what she wants. *(Realizing she's incriminated Ama)* Well, she wants the best for us. Me and Alex. That's all I meant. *(GRACIELA offers her hands.)* Here. Why don't you arrest me instead? I love my Ama. I'd do anything for her, so go ahead. You found her. At Saint Augustine's Cathedral downtown. Well, it was Sunday morning. Before four a.m.? Please. Have pity on her. My mother's practically a *viejita. (Short beat)* Well, we get old fast *en mi barrio. (Beat)* Her going to confession doesn't mean a thing. She goes every week. She always thinks she's got some great sin. She went to confession for breaking the garbage disposal. She went to confession for cheating at poker. She went to confession for taking God's name in vain the day Alex fell in the ring. But who should be confessing here? Maybe God himself should go to confession for taking His sword and piercing it straight through my mother's heart.

(Note: "Viejita" *translates as* "little old lady," *and* "en mi barrio" *means* "in my neighborhood.")*

116

Drawing Down Clio
by Doug Baldwin

Teddie, a mature but madcap woman recently widowed, finds herself lost in a world of personal and emotional isolation following the death of her husband. After a lengthy soul-searching bereavement, she has returned to a high-powered advertising agency and resumed her role as president and chief executive. Here, in darkly tart but sardonic dialogue, Teddie voices the deeper self-knowledge and bah-humbug boredom she experienced during the perfectly miserable Christmas holidays. Her tongue-in-cheek humor is both sadly personal and unexpectedly entangled with questions of her own survival.

TEDDIE: I have just had the worst Christmas of my life. It was torture. Sheer torture. I mean … He's dead. Leo's *been* dead, for weeks, but I just haven't been able to get through the mourning part of it. So, this holiday season, instead of red and green, everything was black. Black black black. Did you know you can actually get black ornaments for your tree? Well, you can. They sell them at the funeral home. Boy, they suck those Christmas lights right out of their sockets. *(Makes a sucking noise.)* Our tree looked like a six-foot black hole. With tinsel. To cheer me up, everybody bought me blouses. *(Models her blouse.)* Ta-da! Seven blouses, size twelve — all black. All wrapped in shiny black paper. It's comforting, in a way: despite being in deep bereavement, I have remained color-coordinated. So, there I am Christmas morning, my first in I-don't-know-how-many years without Leo — slightly sauced, dressed like Darth Vader, lurching around the house, blubbering all over the place. My poor kids kept steering me away from the tree. I think they were afraid I'd be sucked into that black hole. It was really the most miserable holiday you can imagine. Bing Crosby's worst nightmare — a black Christmas. I mean, Santa and the Grim Reaper: what a team.

Tirade

by Mary Louise Wilson

The Actress, a rough-hewn but vulnerable woman of a "certain age," finds herself eclipsed by a younger rival and is forced to accept the painful reality that the theatre can be a quirky, unpredictable, and painful adventure all at the same time. Assuming a somewhat grandiose and menacing manner, with more than a slight note of injury and insult in her voice, the Actress struggles to pull together the shattered strands of an uncertain future. Although the Actress may be celebrating the art of knowing oneself, there is a noticeable tinge of self-doubt and sadness in her definition.

ACTRESS: I don't like to blow my own horn, but I have some standing in the theatre community. I am not exactly chopped liver in this town. People know my work, I know people, people know me. In fact, I was at a peak, an all-time high in my career.

I had just opened in my one-woman show *Tra-La!*, an evening of song and anecdote based on my life in the theatre. You probably saw the reviews? "A benchmark performance," "A comedic watershed," "Pitch-perfect," blah blah blah.

And then this other show opened off-Broadway; *Sick!* A cancer play. And apparently, the lead, Dorothy Dibble, was nude during the entire evening. Well, in the first act she wore a hospital gown with the back open, but in the second act she was nude. And bald. Nevertheless, *Sick!* was a big hit. You can't beat a cancer play. Audiences love it, they love watching somebody spit into a basin and die for two acts.

Nude and bald. That's acting. Fine! I don't begrudge that. To each his own, I say, and hooray for everybody. I was too busy performing in my own hit to pay much attention anyway.

It was just that I didn't necessarily want to hear about her show all the time. Every other minute someone was asking me, "Have you seen *Sick!* yet?" I was still recovering from my opening night when my sister called from Alabama: "I just heard about this wonderful play *Sick!* Have you seen it?" Well of course I hadn't seen it! I was performing *Tra-La!* eight times a week, and in between I had to have complete bed rest! I called my oldest friend in Boston about coming into town to see my show and she said, "OK, but can you get me tickets to *Sick!*?"

And then this other thing started happening: this old theatre queen who lives in my building attacked me in the lobby. "Guess who just moved in down the street?" I started to say I heard Meryl Streep had bought a house nearby when he screamed at me, "Not *her,* Dorothy Dibble!" I arrived at my neighborhood hair salon and Jeffry the stylist hooted, "You just missed Dorothy Dibble!"

Even the doorman. One night as I was leaving the building I distinctly heard Jahmeal the doorman say, "Dorothy Dibble." I grabbed his lapels. "What did you just say?" The poor man has a very thick accent. I let go when I realized he was saying, "Door thing. Jiggle."

But, I mean, why do people think one actress is just dying to hear about another actress, anyway? Is one pipe fitter thrilled to know about another pipe fitter's work?

A Mother's Day Monologue
by Glenn Hascall

This "Mother's Day" original monologue draws a real-life portrait of the heartache, sorrow, and — finally — overwhelming joy of a woman whose sensitive narrative captures her courageous spirit in spite of having suffered a number of traumatic miscarriages and stillborn deaths. The unconquerable optimism and will to survive that she exhibits in the emotional and spiritual journey across the harsh landscape of grief and sorrow comes more clearly into focus when she and her husband adopt a little boy named Cameron.

MOTHER: Do you remember the moment you held your first child in your arms? I do. Such perfect delicate features and eyes that really wanted to focus and a smile that was probably something else. I had dreamed of children and my husband and I had long desired a house full, but miscarriages and stillbirth plagued every attempt.

There were nights I would dream of the faces of children that never lived as they mouthed the word "Mama" — and I awoke in tears, wondering what's wrong with me that I can't bear children. We prayed, we visited doctors, we tried homespun approaches to bearing children … and then came Cameron. A perfect little child — great disposition. Slept through the night almost from the first night we brought him home. We've watched him grow, and so many have noticed features they see in both our son and in us. We smile in a pride that is shared by parents the world over.

My husband does everything with Cameron. He is such a good daddy. Cameron rides on his shoulders and giggles as David throws him in the air and then catches him. I remember the first time David did that, I thought I was going to have a heart attack. Our son completely trusts his daddy — I just try not to watch. Cameron has become such a part of our lives. You know, I often stop at the door of his room and just listen to the even breathing of sound sleep. I remember watching to see his chest rise and fall — just to be sure. Who am I kidding? I did the same thing last night.

But Cameron is on loan to us, you know? We are his parents, but he's not really ours. God has loaned Cameron to us for a while, and we are taking advantage of every moment we can with that little boy. The incredible pain of losing a child still disturbs me from time to time, but then again I have seen the story from the other side. You see, Cameron did not grow in my womb, he grew in my heart. I did not give him birth, but I am his mommy.

I still remember the anguish in Lisa's face as she handed little Cameron to us. She had considered abortion, but somehow miraculously decided to give her baby life — and now David and I are giving him a home. Maybe you have a child that has been driving you nuts — do me a favor — go home today and hug 'em for a while — even if they squirm away. They need it — you need it.

I sometimes wonder what Lisa is doing on Mother's Day. Is she married? Does she have another child? Is she crying as she wraps her arms around thin air remembering her son? If I had a chance to talk to Lisa again, there is so much I would say. Thank you for bearing my son. Thank you for giving him life. Thank you for caring enough for Cameron to share him with us. Happy Mother's Day, Lisa.

Tales from the Tunnel
by Troy Diana and James Valletti

In this original monologue, an aloof Young Girl with a flair for the dramatic has an unsettling experience on the Queens Boulevard, New York City, subway that is puzzling but also sharply humorous. Riding along on a hot, sweltering summer afternoon packed shoulder to shoulder in a crowded subway car, the Young Girl has an uneasy feeling when the lights in the car suddenly go out that something — or someone — is rubbing against her leg … and licking her ankle! A darkly comic psychological melodrama follows until the lights come on again and we realize that the Young Girl's irreverent, funny, and deeply puzzling experience has a surprise happy ending.

YOUNG GIRL: It was a sweltering summer afternoon, sometime back in the 1970s. We'd just left the Queens Boulevard station and were heading towards Roosevelt Avenue — about a fifteen-minute ride. That day I was wearing a dress and sandals, but no stockings — too hot for them. And people were crowded in that car, packed shoulder to shoulder. Luckily, I had a seat. I couldn't move in it, but I had one anyway.

Suddenly, the lights in the car went out. No big deal — it happened all the time. But then I felt something wet drag across my ankle. At first I thought I imagined it, but ohhhh no! I felt it again. It was someone's tongue. I was going to move, but it was crowded and dark — so I had no choice but to stay. I moved my leg, but everywhere I put it the tongue seemed to follow, licking and licking. I tried kicking, but couldn't get rid of it. I didn't want to scream or kick too hard — I knew it would cause a panic. In the dark, rushing toward Roosevelt Avenue, all I could do was picture a guy lying on the floor of the dirty train, getting off on licking my ankle.

I couldn't wait to get to the station to confront this guy and turn him in for this disgusting crime. When the train pulled into the station, the lights flickered on, the doors opened, and the crowd quickly moved off the train. On the floor by my ankle I confronted the culprit: a Seeing Eye dog. I left the train, my moist ankle carrying me away from the scene of the crime.

Don't Breathe on the Job
by Allen Davis III

A highly qualified but financially struggling Puerto Rican Woman is in desperate need to find a job to help support her family. In this disturbing but revealing interview with a prospective corporate employer, we witness a prejudicial parody of the "American Dream," a rude awareness of the role that prejudice continues to play in society. The woman's life and qualifications for the position are unceremoniously examined, questioned and, at last, dismissed by the self-absorbed employer. There is some dark humor here, but the focus is on Puerto Rican self-identity as it is sometimes displaced or distorted by others, and where sense and sensibility seem to shift and blur as expediency dictates.

PUERTO RICAN WOMAN: This is what happened. I am recommended for a secretary job at this big corporation. The man who hires greets me and gives me coffee. He is about to order a pizza which he offers me — no, first he asks, "Do you prefer rice or beans?" and I joke with him that I do not need rice or beans three times a day, but he does not laugh. So he sends out for pizza, extra pepperoni in my honor.

I do not feel comfortable, but this is a good-paying job and I need it. He tells me they have no Spanish employees in the front office, and the big, liberal boss thinks this is a terrible oversight. I tell him, yes it is, and he says, "I thought Puerto Ricans were Puerto Ricans," and I say, oh no, Puerto Ricans are definitely Hispanic. So he thinks for a second and says, "Maybe that's even better. I mean, you're almost an American, right?" He says the big, liberal boss insists on a real Spanish secretary, so I simply say I am real and Spanish, and he replies, "You may be too real. We want someone Spanish, but not too Spanish."

I don't understand, but I need this job badly. My husband's pay is not enough, so I say I will be as Spanish as he wants and that I type ninety words a minute, take shorthand, and am experienced on the Wang. I remark I know I am a little darker than some Hispanics, and he jumps in: "We have no discrimination because of race, religion, or color. We only have discrimination because of oversights. In fact, we prefer the person we hire not to be too light because then she would look and sound like an American, and that wouldn't be fair to the Spanish." I assure him I can improve on my accent, and he says, "Oh no, your accent is perfect. Very believable."

I do not understand any of this. They want a Latino, but they don't want a Latino, but they don't want an American either. He tells me, "Of course, I will need to see your citizenship papers." I remind him I am Puerto Rican. My father was drafted into the Marines. He becomes agitated because he is not sure the big, liberal boss will be convinced a Puerto Rican is a real Spanish-type person without a piece of paper telling him so. I promise him a piece of paper showing that my parents were born in Santurce, Puerto Rico. He asks if it is near San Juan, and I reply it is on the same island. Now he says, "I must have your birth certificate and a list of all the places you and your parents lived. I must make double sure of this." I am getting as nervous as this man, but I say fine, fine, I will get a list together. Does this mean I have the job? He says there should be no problem, but first he must explain to me, "In the front office we don't allow low-cut dresses, stiletto heels, and no long red fingernails." And there I sit in my only Laura Ashley, but he does not see me, so I begin to get angry. He warns me some more: "You must be extra careful not to agitate the men in the office — no long eyelashes, no beauty marks on the bosom." My blood is enraged. I tell him I am here to work, only to work, to do a good job. That is all. "Good," he said, "just watch how you breathe on the job — no heaving chests ..."

Right then the pizza arrives, and before I can think, I lift it off the tray and am about to heave it in his face when I see the sticky cheese and pepperoni dripping on his word processor keys. He is frightened, he is angry, he cringes, he cries, "Oh my god — a spitfire." I do not get the job.

I Never Got to Say Good-Bye
by Lexanne Leonard

This crisp, clear, and often lyrical original monologue features Gabby, a fiercely independent and spirited young girl caught up in a horrific series of tragedies and torn apart from the inside as well as beyond. It is a beautifully drawn portrait evoking the sadness and pathos of a young girl in crisis who finds herself in unexpected situations of real emotional consequence while confronting the harsh realities of life. The complex ethical and moral questions of personal guilt and responsibility explored about some of the most troublesome aspects of the human condition are treated with blunt, riveting honesty that brings the monologue to a harrowing climax ... and is genuinely heartbreaking in its depiction of the bleakness of loss.

GABBY: No one told me we would leave without Bremen. I hated that they made the decision without me. I never got to say good-bye. I didn't care that he was old and not eating. I didn't care that he would wander around the house only to be stopped by a wall or chair, not knowing what to do or how to move around it. No one told me about the pain of letting him go. I hated them. I hated my mom for not saying anything, just sitting there like she always does when there are hard decisions to make. I hated my dad for telling me to be brave.

Brave? My dog was going to die. My only friend. The only living being who didn't care how I cut my hair or what label I wear or how skinny I am. They were going to kill him and I didn't have a say. I hurt too much to be brave. I ran when the vet brought out the needle. I watched the steam from my vomit rise up from the puddle in the parking lot and fade away into the sky. Everything was covered in ice. It was so white and bright from the moon bouncing off the snow that it hurt my eyes.

For a second I squinted at the sparkling ice crystals hanging from the tree branches and thought how lovely they were. But only for a second because my coat was being placed over my shoulders and I heard my father's voice telling me that it was all over and to get in the car. He said it was too cold to be out in the open. My mother reached out with a tissue to wipe off my mouth. I slapped it from her hand.

"Leave me alone," I said as I pushed myself away from them and climbed into the backseat. I cried in the car on the way home and hissed at my mom when she tried to hand me another tissue. I howled at my dad to "Shut up!" when he said "It will make you stronger." He always said stupid things like that when I lost a swim meet or had a hard time learning a new stroke. Or when he made me do the Polar Bear swim with him on New Year's Day and it was so cold in the water that I hurt down to my bones. I hated them both with a passion. I roared at him to stop the car and leave me on the side of the road. I couldn't stand being in the same place with them, yet alone in that ridiculous hybrid my father was so proud of.

I never got to say good-bye. My dad was turning around to say something else profound to me, but I didn't hear it. All I heard was my mom screaming and before I knew it the car was spinning, slamming into things before finally crashing through the ice into the lake. I remember his hands releasing my seat belt, grabbing my shoulders and shoving me through the broken window as if we were in slow motion.

I remember pushing up through the icy water, gasping for air. I remember seeing my mom struggling in the water and me grabbing her from behind and pulling her to shore. Kneeling in the snow, I waited for my dad. The steam rose from my breath into the sky above the trees. Then came the flashing lights. My mother's guttural sobs spit out behind me, but there was no dad coming up through the slush. Ice crystals hung from my hair. Tears ran into my mouth, warm and salty.

Then came the quiet. Shadows of people. Legs moving all around me. Faces appearing in front of me as I pushed them away to watch the cracked ice sloshing against the band of the river. Arms pulling me out of the snow. Voices I couldn't hear asking me questions I didn't understand. Waiting an eternity to see him. The top of his head never coming up.

A blanket wrapped itself around me and something turned me away from the water. I tried to walk. Hands around my shoulders nudged me, trying to push me away from the water, but my feet wouldn't move. A deep voice broke through the silence, "Miss, walk with me." Looking back over my shoulder, I saw flippered feet kick up in the air and disappear beneath the inky liquid. My knees buckled and blackness shrouded over me.

I never got to say good-bye.

Six Views

by Lisa Kirazian

Karen, a courageous and heroic young mother, is slowly dying as she lies in a hospital bed while a dark silence engulfs her. This original monologue is an overpowering portrait of the poignancy and sense of loss each of us must face when we reluctantly take that final, fatal breath. Although Karen has accepted the inescapable truth of her condition, it is unswerving love and compassion for her husband and children that gives her a fleeting glance of unexpected grace and a candid snapshot of death as the natural order of things. Hers is a journey into those dark spaces within the human mind which most of us never unlock until it is our time to face that inevitable reckoning.

KAREN: I kept the suitcase in the closet — and I'd pack a thing here, a thing there, when the kids weren't looking. I didn't want to get the barrage of questions: "Where are you going? How long will you be gone? When will you come back?"

"What do you mean you might not come back? What do you mean you might die? Die? Mommy, are you going to die? Can't they fix what's wrong? Why can't you get better?" All that.

At night, after they went to bed, I cooked weeks' worth of dinners and put them in the freezer, before my energy started going, because I knew that they were going to need something, some reminder of me, some warmth, something from my hands, while I was gone. I started thinking of what Lou's face would look like when he takes the last one out of the freezer. The last meal from his wife — whose cooking he loves. The last sweet taste of her special marinara sauce, which has cumin in it — that's the secret, cumin and sugar. I never told anyone. He'll always think I had some magic going on in there.

And my laundry — I didn't have the heart to do my laundry. I didn't want everything to be so neat and tidy and clean and finished-looking. Because there's nothing that looks like "I'll be back" more than a bag of unwashed laundry, dishes in the sink, a cup of coffee half-drunk by the computer that you can microwave later, a book left open on the armchair. I noticed all these things. I kept them that way on purpose, because I thought that just maybe if I surrounded myself with details like that, with little pockets of possibility, then maybe they'd force a change in destiny. Maybe the powers that be would look at the laundry and the coffee cup and the dishes and think, "We can't take her yet — she still has a lot to do."

But they didn't. They took me, and they took me on a day I didn't even have a chance to say good-bye to my family. They were on the way. Stuck in traffic because Lou went the way he always goes, the way I always tell him not to go: the carpool lane. It always seems like it's going to be faster but it never is. So I could feel it happening, the breath slowing down, the nurses fussing around me, my eyes closing, even though I could hear all the honking and the morning rush hour outside. It all started fading, and I couldn't do anything about it. I wanted to see them, to kiss them, but then more than anything I wanted to go to sleep, and the sleep came over me and over me and filled me and finished me.

CHAPTER 6
A TIME OF CYNICISM

"Cynicism is an unpleasant way of saying the truth."
— Lillian Hellman, *The Little Foxes*

In a time of cynicism, the authors strip away the pathos that masks their characters' human frailties and, in the process, make a significant statement about the world in which we live. Serious and wise with a dash of fresh homespun philosophy, these character sketches are irresistibly human observations that frequently speak in blunt, uninhibited images that are alive and throbbing — and we see through their eyes a cynical world filled with characters struggling to come to grips with their own fragile survival.

There is an uncommon, sometimes satirical or whimsical, sense of sparkling humor that reveals a mix of fantasy and reality that shapes the lives of these characters. Secrets surface, friendships unravel, and echoes of festering jealousy or resentment catch you off guard. Character attitudes being twisted and spun also add a deft brush stroke to complete the portraits.

Just as their world is changing around them, the characters experience unexpected moments that are both celebratory and caustic. There is an intoxicating mix of pathos and humor that is heartfelt as the characters struggle to realize their dreams in spite of unforeseen obstacles. Anger, regrets, and self-deception slowly fade as the characters wrestle with their own demons and try to make sense of their lives ... if only to quiet the cries of their shattered dreams in a time of cynicism.

Ruined
by Lynn Nottage

*A dark and damp rainforest bar and shabby brothel in the civil-war-
torn Congo is the setting for this raw and gripping Pulitzer Prize
drama of women "ruined" by rape and torture as government soldiers
and rebel forces wantonly abuse them at will. Salima, a young wife and
mother abducted from her home by rebel soldiers and forced into
prostitution, stands Center Stage, bruised and dirty. Her face is a
harrowing mask of shock and numbness like that of small children who
have seen horrors they should never have to witness. Moving slowly
backward in time, Salima recalls the brutality of her capture.*

SALIMA: It was such a clear and open sky. This splendid bird, a
peacock, had come into the garden to taunt me, and was showing off its
feathers. I stooped down and called to the bird: "Wssht, Wssht." And I
felt a shadow cut across my back, and when I stood four men were
there over me, smiling wicked schoolboy smiles. "Yes?" I said. And the
tall soldier slammed the butt of his gun into my cheek. Just like that. It
was so quick, I didn't even know I'd fallen to the ground. Where did
they come from? How could I not have heard them?

One of the soldiers held me down with his foot. He was so heavy,
thick like an ox and his boot was cracked and weathered like it had
been left out in the rain for weeks. His boot was pressing my chest and
the cracks in the leather had the look of drying sorghum. His foot was
so heavy, and it was all I could see as the others ... "took" me. My baby
was crying. She was a good baby. Beatrice never cried, but she was
crying, screaming. "Shhhh," I said. "Shhhh." And right then ... *(Closes
her eyes.)* A soldier stomped on her head with his boot. And she was
quiet. *(A moment)* Where was everybody? *Where was everybody?*

But they still took me from my home. They took me through the
bush. "She is for everyone, soup to be had before dinner," that is what
someone said. They tied me to a tree by my foot, and the men came
whenever they wanted soup. I make fires, I cook food, I listen to their
stupid songs, I carry bullets, I clean wounds, I wash blood from their
clothing, and, and, and ... I lay there as they tore me to pieces, until I

was raw ... five months. Five months. Chained like a goat. These men fighting ... fighting for our liberation. Still I close my eyes and I see such terrible things. Things I cannot stand to have in my head. How can men be this way?

Night Luster
by Laura Harrington

Roma, a sensitive and single young singer and songwriter in her twenties, is a dreamer and hopeless romantic who has lost the ability to separate the real world from the realm of dreams and fantasy. Used and abused by the parade of men who have passed through her life, Roma looks for self-forgiveness — the light within herself — and a sense of purpose that will give new meaning to a future life full of hope and love. Here, she is speaking to her best friend, Mink, but it is the unspoken drama behind her words that casts a shadow on the limits of her desire and the possibilities for future happiness.

ROMA: I don't think people see me. I get this feeling sometimes like I'm invisible or something. I can be standing there in a room and I'm talking and everything, and it's like my words aren't getting anywhere, and I look down at myself and *Jesus*, sometimes my body isn't getting anywhere either. It's like I'm standing behind a one-way mirror and I can see the guys and I can hear the guys, but they can't see me and they can't hear me. And I start to wonder if maybe I'm ugly or something, like maybe I'm some alien species from another planet and I don't speak the language and I look totally weird. But I don't know this, you see, because on this other planet I had this really nice mother who told me I was beautiful and that I had a voice to die for because she loved me so much, not because it was true. And I arrive here on earth and I'm so filled with her love and her belief in me that I walk around like I'm beautiful and I sing like I have a voice to die for. And because I'm so *convinced* and so strange and so *deluded*, people *pretend* to listen to me ... because they're being polite or something — or maybe they're afraid of me. And at first I don't notice because I sing with my eyes closed. But then one day I open my eyes and I find out I'm living in a world where nobody sees me and nobody hears me.

(Beat) I'm just lookin' for that one guy who's gonna hear *me*, see *me* ... really take a chance. I hear *them*. I'm listening so hard I hear promises when somebody's just sayin' hello ... Jesus, if anybody ever heard what I've got locked up inside of me ... I'd be a *star*.

Baggage
by Sam Bobrick

Mitzi Cartwright, a free-spirited and offbeat woman whose irreverent sense of humor and outlandish strangeness always adds a raucous note of fun to any social occasion, is visiting her friend, Phyllis, who is single and trying to recover from yet another disappointing breakup. Here, Mitzi puts a sharp and snappy spin on "friendly advice" as she strolls around sharing her views on how to spice up an apartment as well as a romance. Her comic rant is a nonstop roller coaster ride of comic wit and social observation that is irresistible — but unlikely to pave Phyllis's path to true love and happiness.

MITZI: You know what this apartment needs? Adventure. Excitement. The way it is now, it's too perfect, too ordinary. Everything is where it's supposed to be. There's no mystery, no romance. You expect a chair there, there's a chair there. You expect a table there, there's a table there. The windows have drapes, the floor has a rug, the walls have pictures. Just what is the statement? There is none. You know what I did to my living room? I said to hell with this everyday plebeian thinking. I threw caution to the wind. First I got rid of everything. Emptied the entire room. Then I had the walls painted chartreuse. For seating I scattered large fluffy pillows all around. Then in the center of the room I put in a large fish pond and filled it with a dozen or so large koi fish. With whatever space was left I filled it with plastic pink flamingos and large potted palms decorated with lights in motion. Well, now you walk into my living room and it's an explosion. People actually lose their balance when they first enter. My insurance company made me put in a hand rail near the front door. But I love what it's saying. "Here resides a woman dancing to her own music. A

131

bold, daring woman. A trendsetter." Sure, a few people have thrown up when they first come in, but at least I know it stirred their imagination. I can't wait for you to come over and see it. Just be sure to bring some Dramamine.

The Pain and the Itch
by Bruce Norris

In this satire on the nature of open-mindedness and tolerance, Carol, an affluent and privileged middle-class woman with old wounds she has been nursing for years, shares her views on class and race to her family on Thanksgiving. Slowly and quietly, Carol peels away layers of deep-seated mistrust and misconceptions about some of the elemental differences about diversity and stereotype role-playing. Her arguments are passionately framed and focused, but there is an undeniable tone in her voice that suggests denial and resentment may lie just beneath the surface.

CAROL: Let me ask you something. I was watching a documentary the other night on PBS. I don't know if you watch PBS. I'm a subscriber. And sometimes I volunteer for the pledge drives. But mostly I think what else is there to watch? I mean, really, well, there's the Discovery Channel. But ninety-nine percent of what's on television, I just look at it and I … I don't *disapprove,* I mean, more power to all that. Diversity and everything. Diversity is so important. But it's like with *junk food,* isn't it? I say to my first graders, if *all* you eat is junk food, then you can hardly expect to feel good about yourself. And you know, I was showing them a wonderful program all about families around the world, from each continent, and when they got to the tribesmen in New Guinea, who wear very little clothing, just some leaves and … *gourds,* but it's the *tropics,* after all, well, some of the children started to *laugh.* And you know that just upset me so much. So I said to them, well now, let's all just *think* for a minute. Let's think how *you* would like to be laughed at. If you went to New Guinea right now, dressed in your *American* clothes? That wouldn't be very nice, would it? How do we ever expect to reach out to new cultures and embrace new ideas if all we can do is *laugh? (Back to her main point)* And plus. Bill Moyers is so wonderful. So I was watching the documentary, which was all about *Genghis Khan.* Did you see that?

Stain
by Tony Glazer

This darkly bleak and exceedingly painful monologue explores the devastating human impact of a family's "dark secret." Theresa, a mature woman struggling to break through a web of grief and bitter disappointment, shares a deeply personal confession about her deceased husband As she struggles with emotionally charged memories and her own conscience, Theresa sketches a vivid self-portrait of a woman trapped in an unreal and yet hauntingly real past ... both at the same time.

THERESA: When he was alive — this was years ago — we had a mouse problem. We were pretty sure it was just the one mouse unless they had it worked out in shifts — I'm not sure how mice plan these things. Samuel, my husband Samuel, decided to buy a glue trap and set it where we normally saw the little brown thing creep about. I had heard glue traps were cruel so I was a little tentative about it, but Samuel insisted it was just a rodent and it had to be done. Anyway, one night, I awoke to hear this ... squeaking sound. I looked for Samuel but he wasn't in bed, so I put on my robe and followed the squeaking sounds and I found Samuel in his pajamas hunched over the glue trap that he had cut open and, with a spoon, very tenderly separating this wide eyed, brown, little mouse from the trap. And the mouse squeaked and squeaked, but Samuel pressed on, little by little, delicately but firmly freeing this little, helpless mouse. I sat there and watched him — it seemed like hours. When he finally got the mouse free, patches of its fur were stripped away. You could see parts of its skin exposed and raw. He opened the front door and the mouse very slowly, very gingerly limped its way out of our house. I watched Samuel stand there for a while, looking out the open door, watching the mouse hobble away. I snuck back to the bedroom, and he never mentioned the moment to me.

We didn't have a mouse problem after that — our little friend was either the only one or word traveled fast. But I never forgot that. I never forgot how tender and sensitive, how deeply caring he was. That's how I remember him now: a warm, sensitive, deeply caring man who was raping our daughter. That's what's hard for me, Thomas.

Funny
by Christyna Belden

This bittersweet original monologue spiced with a grim tragic dimension is an incisive portrait of a mercurial Nameless Woman who has hidden years of emotional and physical abuse behind a mask of satirical humor. The mask, however, is only a faint reflection of her own grimly painful struggle to survive in a world that refuses to acknowledge her existence. Speaking in richly evocative, pungent language, the Nameless Woman finally confronts her peers and those who have wrongly judged her as she reveals an indomitable spirit and humanity that reminds us the characters who refuse to pity themselves are the ones who most rouse it in us.

NAMELESS WOMAN: You don't know me, and you probably never will. No, please don't stop and stare. I don't like it when you get too close. For my entire life people pass me by, and now I am used to it. Anything else would confuse me. OK, OK, I actually have a lot of "friends." You see, I make people laugh. I'm the "funny" girl. Because when people are busy laughing, they are not thinking about what is going on in my life. They just think, "Man is *she* funny" ... and funny is good.

There are some people that say I'm too funny, that I need to grow up and take life serious. What they don't know is that my life has been serious enough without their help. Sure it is easy to look at me and judge me at face value, but they don't know the real me on the inside. There are others that think I am bad, bad for myself, bad for those around me. I hope not. I never thought of myself as being bad, just funny. Look, I know I'm not anyone's idea of the perfect person, but what's wrong with laughing? Isn't there enough misery in life? Laugh it up, that's what I say.

I am more comfortable when you ignore the real me, the one I never let you see. I keep her hidden where she is safe. Because I realized a long time ago that if I let you really get to know her, you have the power to hurt her, and that isn't funny. I have been hurt before, and I wanted to die; and maybe on the inside I did a little. Do you know what that is like? To find out that the world isn't safe like you thought it was? I found that out early in life. I wanted the world to be a safe place, but it didn't work out that way. Do you think I wanted my life like this? Do you think I wanted to lose my innocence? Well, it's not a safe world at all. So you are better off to just laugh at it ... it's much safer.

Oh, I know there are people that don't approve of me and others that only want me around for the entertainment and hey, that's OK. Because if I don't have your approval, you leave me alone and that's the way I want it. I don't like it when you are in my life trying to figure me out. It bothers me, and I don't want you getting too close. Close isn't safe. You get too close and then you can see things I don't want you to see; secrets about my life that I have hidden from you. Now I know that you will assume what everyone else does, my secrets are bad things I've done. But what if I told you that my secrets were bad things that happened to me? Would it make a difference? Would you accept me then? But you see, I don't want you to accept me because you feel sorry for me. I want you to accept me because you like me ... for me.

Sensitivity

by Lisa Soland

Michelle, a mature but quirky woman who has always had a special gift for experiencing the emotions that other people were feeling, is struggling to understand the harrowing and heartbreaking loss of a man she recently started dating, and who died suddenly before they had even shared their first innocent kiss. Here, Michelle voices the flood of intertwining doubts and fears that still linger in her memory of that fateful first date and the deep sense of personal guilt and remorse that continues to plague her.

MICHELLE: I've always had this ... sensitivity. *(Beat)* When I was a kid, I could pretty much feel what other people were feeling. I could feel it so strongly that my own feelings, what I was feeling, were pretty much put on the back burner. After two disastrous, long-term relationships, I decided that I was going to face whatever it was that was keeping me from ... living out the life I was supposed to live. *(Beat)* I found this therapist, and he was good. And he sat there quiet ... mostly, for about two years. Quiet helps. *(Beat)*

But anyway, during this time I gathered up the courage to sign up with this online dating service. They set me up with this guy, thirty, I guess, and we met for coffee. That's what you do. You meet for coffee and decide whether or not you want to continue the date from there. Well, we did. And when we walked back to our cars, I remember standing by his SUV and thinking to myself that he wanted to kiss me. I could feel it. But he didn't. So after a few more minutes we said good-bye and I went home. When I walked in the door, there's this email waiting for me from him, saying how he had wanted to kiss me. And I wrote him back and said, "Well ... you should have!" *(Beat)* Anyway, it was cute. So a couple of days later, I go on my computer and Steve is online, so I instant message him and say, "Hey, you bum. What are you doing home from work?" And he wrote back, only it's not him. It's his friend, and he tells me that Steve was killed in a car accident driving back from Las Vegas. Just like that. Gone. The next few days were weird. I started sensing Steve around me. I could feel him somehow in my chest. My heart, maybe. One day, I'm back in with my therapist and suddenly I feel Steve in the room ... this amazingly deep sadness, and I see ... his SUV rolling over and over and over and I feel all this confusion and ... *(She shakes her head and stops.)*

Anyway, instead of ignoring it and trying to continue on with my session, I decide to take a chance and tell my therapist what's going on. He listens, and says, "Tell him to go away." I looked at my therapist and I said, "Can I do that? Can I really just tell him to go away?" And he said, "Yes, you can." *(Beat)* So, I did. And he left. And the pain left. No more sadness. No more tumbling cars. And I've been telling things that hurt to leave ever since.

Sleeping Dogs
by Philip Osment

This powerful monologue explores the deeply buried religious prejudice and mistrust that reached a small, remote village during the civil war in the former Yugoslavia and stripped away the veneer of religious harmony that had existed for some time between Christians and Muslims. Sabina, a devout and caring Muslim mother, has sent her daughter along with the other young children of the village away to safety ... but along the route, the bus is stopped by a group of Christian militia and all the Muslim children are slaughtered. Sabina now cradles her dead child as she weaves a tender narrative of regret and loss.

SABINA: Still warm,
She's still warm.
While I was measuring out the flour
She was sitting chatting to her friend.
While I was weighing out the butter,
Armed men stepped in front of the bus.
While I was mixing them together,
They shot the driver and got on board.
While I was adding sugar
They separated my daughter from her friend
Lined her up with the other Muslims on the bridge.
While I was cracking eggs
Someone held a knife to her neck.
While I was stirring them in,
He slit her throat.
As I poured the mixture into the tin
She died.
Feel her,
She's still warm.
(She drops the knife onto the ground. They go to comfort her.)
Leave me.

New York Actor
by John Guare

Several self-absorbed actors are relaxing in a dimly lit bar, glibly reflecting on the true measure of their theatrical success and failure — their own and that of their fellow thespians. The actors gallop along with hilarious — sometimes banal — banter about roles won and opportunities lost that is by turns both heartening and saddening. The Critic's Wife, a rather dour woman with an air of grand hauteur, seated at a nearby table with her husband, has been a keen listener of the woeful tales drifting her way and seizes the opportunity to voice her own opinions on the theatre!

CRITIC'S WIFE: I hate the theater. I hate the theater more than anything. I hate the contempt with which the little man at the door rips your ticket. I hate the little glossy program the usher hands you filled with pieces raving how wonderful the theater is. I hate it when I sit and look at the curtain on the stage. The dread of what lifting it is going to reveal. I hate it when there isn't a curtain. That? That's what I'm going to have to look at all night? I hate the people around me. I hate it when the audience applauds actors the moment they come out on stage. I hate seeing the makeup line at the actor's neck. I hate the artificial way actors talk. I hate the way they signal with their hands and mouths and bodies that a laugh line is coming up. I hate the way they freeze to hold for a laugh that never comes from me. I hate it when they burst into song. Most of all I hate it when actors look into the audience and talk to me as if I was their friend. I don't want actors revealing their innermost secrets, their so-called motives, their ludicrous hopes, laying out their noble dreams whose only purpose is to be crushed. Somebody else wrote their shoddy little secrets anyway. I hate playwrights. I hate directors. I hate the lighting. I hate the scenery.

I wanted to marry a war correspondent. I thought I did. We met in Beirut during the war. In those days, he was a stringer for a weekly news magazine. I was on a TV crew. The two of us dreamed of a future of war zones, battlefields, civil insurrection. Fixing meals on hot plates in Mideast hotel rooms, making love in Israel as bombs go off over our heads, plaster falling down on us in joyous affirmation of our life. A tent in Bosnia. Watching him type his cogent reports on a beat-up portable Olivetti while I stayed back in the narrow cot, looking at him with pride. Smoking non-filters. Dreaming of the Spanish Civil War. Instead we came back to New York. Some chance of a lifetime. I'm held prisoner by a deranged kleptomaniac actor under a table looking for my keys in a show biz bar, lined with posters of flops. Everything's a flop. *Hamlet's* a flop. *The Oresteia's* a flop. *Hedda Gabler's* a flop. *The Cherry Orchard's* a flop. *Death of a Salesman's* a flop. Me? Me? What am I?

Let's Not Talk about Men
by Carla Cantrelle

Gwen, a feisty and salty-tongued young woman desperately trying to find a meaningful relationship with her dream Prince Charming, has become skeptical and disillusioned by the dating game ritual of attraction and seduction. Trapped in a love/hate nightmare world of failed romance, Gwen voices almost uncontrollable anger and rage to a married friend as she relives very real and nagging episodes that have poisoned her outlook on romance and suggest she has finally accepted the reality that her dating destiny is something over which she now has complete control.

GWEN: Today I hate all of them. Especially the ones I don't know. Them most of all. Because soon I'll know them and they'll do something to make me hate them. But since I don't know them, I don't know what that horrible thing will be. I won't be prepared. And because I'm an idiot, I'll think that everything will be different with them. Because they're new. And I don't know them. At least if you know them, you kind of know where the land mines are. You're married. That's a whole different mine field. Dating. Gack. You think you're blithely strolling through the park but it's really the demilitarized zone, and poorly defined at that. Then *pow!* One misplaced reference to some movie that reminds him of his last girlfriend! No warning. Kaplooey! Or one too many, "Does this make me look fat?" Wham! I just hate them. In fact, I don't even want to think about them. Just once, I'd like to get through a day without even mentioning them. Let's make a pact. For this brunch, let's not talk about men!

Local Nobody
by Nicole Pandolfo

Gina, a comic and free-spirited young woman, idolizes the iconic pop star Cher but appears unaware that her own destiny is something over which she has control. A cocaine pill addict whose window on the world is the local Lou's bar, she is a delightful comic oddball with lively wit and biting humor to match her gut-level directness and simplicity. Here, she launches into an increasingly frenetic conversation with Sal, who she meets at the local bar, and reveals a telling measure of what may lie behind her drug-induced delusions.

GINA: What are you drinking? Straight, this early in the day? I usually like to start with something light like a chardonnay or a rum and coke, you know? If I start with the straight hard booze I'll be wasted by lunch, and then I'll do something stupid like forget to eat the rest of the day. It's actually a pretty good diet. Like if you're trying to lose weight. I love whiskey though. A lot. Too much even. I can get kinda out of control when I drink it. Well, when I drink a lot of it. I think it messes with my brain chemistry or something. Just like how people say they get crazy when they drink tequila, I'm like that with whiskey. Yeah, I shouldn't drink whiskey. *(Pause)* Can you believe it's this cold out now? Like, shouldn't it be spring? Or at least above freezing. Is it just me or was this winter the worst in history? I mean, pretty much everyone I know is depressed. I'm too anxious to be depressed. Are you depressed? Wouldn't it be cool if you could kill yourself, like for a week? Or maybe even just a weekend. Just to take a break. I'm talking about a vacation. Well, since I can't afford a vacation, I think temporary suicide would be an interesting alternative. As long as it was temporary. It's just a fantasy.

A Legacy for the Mad
by Don Nigro

Senta, an amusing but seemingly mysterious young woman who works in a music store during the day, is having an amorous affair with Rupert, a charming and playful young man. The star-crossed lovers rendezvous by breaking into the local zoo at night, where Senta routinely drives Rupert mad with lust. In this episode, Senta confesses that she was once married and shares the sad but enthralling tale of her husband's accidental death. As she struggles to make coherent sense of her frustration and rage, Senta opens a uniquely personal window on her journey of pain and suffering.

SENTA: It was late one night. He was coming home in a wagon full of sheep, up the steepest part of the hill, in the cold. The path was icy. The horse was startled by an owl. The wagon turned over, the sheep spilled out, and he struck his head on a stone. He was killed instantly. Then came the reading of the will. There was a bowl of lemons on the table. A clock was ticking. It took me a moment to fully take in what I was hearing. He had left us nothing. He left everything to the state asylum for the insane. Every penny. Nothing for me. Nothing for the children. He left every penny to the insane. I asked myself, why would he do this? Who did he know that was mad? Nobody in the family was mad. They were stupid, but they weren't mad. Yet he left everything to the state mental hospital. It was the only crazy thing he ever did in his life, except for marrying me. We were left with no money. No visible means of support. I was forced into a life of selling grand pianos to marching bands. But that wasn't the worst part. The worst part was trying to understand why. What was he thinking? You live with somebody. You believe you know them. You don't know anything. They might as well be invaders from Uranus. Why the mad? Why leave everything to the mad? I searched through his papers, his correspondence. Nothing. No clues. Did he fear he was going mad? Did he hide it from us, all those years, those of us who believed that we knew him, believed he loved us? What was going on in his head? I thought and thought and thought about it. But the truth is, you don't know anybody. And the people you think you know the best are the biggest strangers of all because you have the most profound illusions about them and the deepest need to perpetuate those illusions at any cost. You make up stories in your head about who people are, why they do things. But you never really know. Most of the pieces are missing from the puzzle. All you're left with, in the end, are a box of disconnected fragments, a room full of old saxophones.

Beauty on the Vine
by Zak Berkman

Lauren Chickering, a brash and abrasive yet fast-rising star in talk radio with a devoted legion of Hannah Montana generation followers, was murdered before she could give full voice to her most controversial views on politics, feminism or religion. The radio station, however, plans to capitalize on Lauren's popularity by hosting a series of "The Best of Lauren Chickering" repeat broadcasts to her devoted listeners. Lauren's provocative fusing of psychological, political, and social themes in this episode is rife with accusations and recriminations that will either engage or enrage the listening audience.

LAUREN: I was at the grocery store and a fat woman walked by me. Very fat with a bad dye job, black spandex jogging shorts, too much eye shadow — she wore a red T-shirt with big lettering that said "All American Mom." No irony. She was mad proud of being who she was: fat, ugly, poorly dressed. There are a lot of these people in our country. Thinking it's OK to be lazy and stupid. How did we get this way? ... Have we been so brainwashed by the liberal elite telling us we're all equal — that we think it's OK now to be fat slobs? It's this kind of thinking that's destroying America — all those do-gooders on the Left, with their arsenal of guilt trips and obsessions with empathy — they've taken away the meaning of greatness. They've made the mediocre and even the evil ... acceptable. But they're wrong. We're *not* equal. We're not all the same ... Those poor and disenfranchised suicide bombers are *still* terrorists. Those child-abused serial killers on death row are *still* murderers. And that fat mom is *still* going to die of heart disease or diabetes when she's fifty, leaving her kids with a legacy of resentment and medical bills. Empathy is useless. Some of us *are* better. Am I right? ... Call me.

Other People
by Christopher Shinn

A couple of young East Village artist roommates in New York City are getting ready to celebrate Christmas ... but tensions quickly surface when their invited guests arrive. Petra, the eccentric and earthy roommate who is a poet and part-time stripper at a local nightclub, has invited one of her customers — a kind, lonely investment banker who would rather talk to Petra than see her strip — to join the celebration. In this rambling bucolic speech, no doubt inspired by a few cocktails, Petra struggles to define herself to her gentleman friend by recalling an incident that gave her a renewed sense of meaning and purpose in life.

PETRA: OK. OK, I'm a freshman in college. A dorm, like a prison, falling apart, roaches, like rats in a lab we are, OK? My roommate is — Dominican or something — and one night she makes this big greasy pot of fish, in this very greasy yellow sauce, and she leaves it simmering on the stove. She goes out to meet her boyfriend. I go into the kitchen. I open the pot. Me. And it looks like sewage. A huge — ridiculous this pot is. And I take out a spoon and think: I'll try this. And I do. I take another bite. Another. And I know, I am a rational being. I know she's cooked this for her boyfriend, they'll be back soon — the whole pot. All of it. And I run into the bathroom and I sit there. I'm numb. I put my hand into my mouth, OK? And I'm covered there in — fish — covered — I look — a ghoul — green, literally — and I'm thinking: *What?* Because I know enough to know this is not normal or healthy in any way and I want to know: *Why?*

Why would I have done this? Why do I feel this way? What in the world — literally, what in the world — in which I find myself living, what at this point in history, what could make a person feel this unbearable sadness and think these terrible thoughts? These thoughts: *I will never be loved. I cannot live in this world.* You see? Because — because my roommate is going to come home and say, Where is the fish, and the only answer is, Petra ate it. Petra ate the fish. And how can I go on? How can I go on without — and I know — that there are people who do not ask this question — because to know — is too much. Because society does not afford them the opportunity to know. Because they are in a constant state of *desire* and desire, *want,* inhibits a consciousness. To become conscious you must stifle yourself, resist your impulses. Not that I had this language then. But I knew; I decided. I decided next time I would not eat the fish. No matter what. No matter what pain that caused me I would put the fork down and place the lid on the pot.

Bad Boys
by Eve Ensler

In this excerpt, the internationally acclaimed playwright offers a fictional monologue inspired by stories told by young girls around the world. Here, a Young Girl confronts the complex issue of defining herself in a world full of confusion and contradiction. She is a wayward soul whose failure to find a meaningful role in life has left her hopelessly lonely, at the mercy of peer pressure and vulnerable to an attraction for "bad boys," who offer the promise of a lifestyle that is fast, fierce, and fun.

YOUNG GIRL: *(New York, New York)*
I like bad boys
It's the danger
He goes to boarding school
He's a darker person
Sort of like me
We're both troubled
I'm better at hiding it
I cut myself
Trying to find something I'm good at
My father is very successful

High expectations
I fail them a lot
I'm not the person they want me to be
My mother wants a perfect family
I don't believe in perfection
Perfect in my mother's world:
Straight As
Super thin
Being intelligent and happy
Really good at everything
I don't know who I am
Cutting myself
Trying to control
Everything crashing down on me
It became a release
I gave my mother a poem
She sent me to a shrink
My shrink
Gave me a rubber band
To put on my wrist
Rather than cutting I snap myself

Mom wants me to be a model
She weighs me every day
She weighs herself twice a day
Her older sister was a model
And she was fat
She's been monitoring my weight since
I was in the 7th grade.
I tell her I don't want to be a model
She says I need to lose pounds
I started to make myself throw up just
So my mother would leave me alone.
My best friend shoots Ritalin to lose weight
Everyone pretends they have ADD

You get extra time on the tests
And you do better which will
Get you into an Ivy League college
I feel absolutely alone in the world
The things my mother would like to change about me:
I'm disorganized
I wear big boots in summer
Have grungy vintage clothing
I listen to weird loud music
I feel a connection with Sylvia Plath
I cut my own hair
Hacked my bangs into pieces
She flipped out
She wants me in Ralph Lauren sweaters

My boyfriend went through rough times
He has his own blog
Yesterday he got grounded
He spray painted a bomb on his bedroom wall
His parents got divorced
He hates his new apartment
He's very angry
Angry at his father for leaving his mother
Angry at the new stupid place where they are living
He is not the most handsome boy
But he's troubled
Like me.

Neverland
by Michael Edan

This dark and disquieting original monologue sketches a disturbing and heart-wrenching portrait of the passionate confusion and shattered dreams of a Teenage Girl who tells the tragic story from her own point of view. Here, she addresses her bewildered parents about the anger, loneliness, and loss that poisoned her life with terribly painful and fatal results for those closest to her heart. It is an absorbing story of the troubled times experienced by many vulnerable adolescents whose innocence, loyalty, and trust are betrayed by others and who sadly, as their resistance crumbles, make a numbing decision that will catch everyone who loves them by surprise.

TEENAGE GIRL: You can't figure it out, can you? You're still too much in shock. We taught her better. What on earth would make her do it? *(Beat)*

You're so clueless. You can't see past your own fantasy. If it wasn't so sad I'd laugh. I don't know why I'm even talking to you now, you won't hear a word I say. I guess it's a final effort to get through to you just how desperate I was. You're going to blame yourselves, of course. If we hadn't done this, if we'd only done that. And that's just crap. Don't you know that? Just more fantasy. What's important is for you to understand, and there's no way I can make you understand. And it's so damn frustrating! *(Slight beat)*

It was just all so ... ugly. I was ugly. The world was ugly. I wanted it to be beautiful and it wasn't. It's supposed to be beautiful and it isn't. I remember when I was a little girl you telling me how beautiful I was. I don't know when I stopped believing that. Maybe it was at Cheryl's birthday pool party when I wore my new swimsuit and the other kids laughed. Or maybe when the girls in 8th grade, who I thought were my friends, decided I was the next person to tweet lies about. Or maybe when Uncle Henry and I were alone after a church social and he put his hand inside my blouse. Maybe it doesn't matter. All I know is the world turned ugly. No one has anything nice to say about anyone else. I could see beauty sometimes, but it was outside. I couldn't really touch it. I couldn't feel it. I could only long for it. Like Neverland, that song you used to sing to me. Remember? Sometimes I'd lie in bed at night and feel the wanting of it so much that my whole body hurt from not having it, and all I could do was cry myself to sleep. Can you understand any of this? *(Slight beat)*

Can you understand what it's like to be in a tunnel that never ends? To believe things can't change for the better? That there's no hope. But it's not your fault. I don't know that it's anyone's fault. It's just how things are. And I'm seeing you looking at me in the casket. You look so

147

lost. And I don't know how to get through to you. How to make you hear me. To let you know ... I'm sorry.

Chocolate Cake
by Mary Gallagher

In this thought-provoking and timely monologue, two "secret gorgers" meet in a hotel room while attending a women's conference. Annmarie, a simple country mouse and compulsive overeater married to a dull mechanic, sees her own probable future if she doesn't change her eating habits ... but lacks the will power to reevaluate her food fixation — or her life — while contending with a mean-spirited husband and a strained marriage. In this tasty confession, Annmarie offers a first-hand glimpse of comfort food compulsion to Delia, her sister binger, and we learn more about the curse of food addiction and what it means to be a secret gorger.

ANNMARIE: Well ... I — I put on a lot of weight ... after I married Robbie. But I never can seem to stay on a diet more than a day or two. I mean, there's Robbie all the time ... and when I have to cook pork chops and hash browns and biscuits and applesauce for him, it seems so dumb to just sit there watching him eat — hearing him chew — while I'm playing with carrot sticks ... especially when he keeps telling me how tasty everything is and what a great little cook I am. Most of the time, he never says a word about my cooking. Just when I'm on a diet. At least it seems like that ... So then, even if I make it through dinner and TV, which is real hard, with Robbie drinking beer and eating snacks ... when we get in bed, every time, here comes Robbie in his pj's with a great big root beer float. He has this mug he got in high school football that says *"Spuds."* That was his nickname in high school, because he loved potatoes. I even call him Spuds sometimes still ... for fun, you know. Anyway, he always uses that great big mug when he makes a root beer float. So there I am in bed, in my see-through nightie, with my hair fluffed up and all ... and he gets in bed right beside me and starts making noises. Like "mmmmm."

So I say, "Robbie, you're just mean." And Robbie says, "Come on, Annie, you know you hate this diet stuff. And you don't need it. You look good, you look like a woman. You're always beautiful to me." I say, "Well, you sure don't act like it." Then he says, "Come on, Annie." And he eats his root beer float. And then he goes to sleep.

And then ... I lie there — as long as I can stand it — and then I get up and put my bathrobe on — the old one with the holes. And I go in the kitchen, and I make myself a great big root beer float. It's twice as big as Robbie's. I make it in the orange juice pitcher. And I eat the whole thing standing up right there at the counter. And then I work my way back through the day. I eat whatever Robbie left at dinner, and whatever I didn't have for lunch because it was too fattening, and whatever I skipped at breakfast ... and then I work my way through the refrigerator and the cupboards. I eat every single thing I can get my hands on that I shouldn't eat. Peanut butter and banana sandwiches! And taco chips and sour cream dip! And fried potato sticks! And Pop-Tarts! And Frosted Flakes right out of the box! And Oreos that I dip in Cool Whip! And sticky buns! And Girl Scout cookies that are still half frozen from the freezer! And then I realize that I'm eating things that I don't even like! Things that taste terrible! Stale Cheese Doodles, and hard marshmallows, and moldy coffee cake! And baking chocolate! And old nasty Easter candy that's all stuck together! And those little flower decorations that you put on birthday cakes! I mean, I don't care! I just eat everything! Everything! Everything that's bad.

Enigma
by Carolyn Carpenter

In this provocative and yet insightful original monologue, Kayla, a strong-willed but sensitive young woman whose childhood was punctuated with jeers and taunts because of her obesity, has undergone a miraculous transformation in recent years and just now been selected to the top ten of the Miss U.S.A. beauty pageant. Although not a top five finalist for the coveted title, Kayla has taken that final step in reconciling the hurt and humiliations of her childhood. Here, she recalls the arduous journey of accepting the inescapable truth of her early condition and the glimpses of self-discovery and unexpected moments of grace that gave her another chance to overcome bitterness and despair with compassion and hope.

KAYLA: Before being crowned Miss Texas U.S.A., I lost one hundred and eighty-nine pounds! I've been fat my whole life! Luckily I don't have a medical condition like a thyroid problem. Obesity does not run in my family. I simply had a mother who fed me pork rinds and milk shakes for breakfast. When the kids at school called me "Kayla the Whale-a," Mama helped me drown my sorrows in pound cake with extra chocolate sauce.

But the pageantry changed everything. Once I saw myself in a bathing suit on television, it was easy to swap Twinkies for a treadmill. Now I am the founder of a motivational program entitled, "Freeing the Fatso Within." Kayla the Whale-a was not my only label in grade school. Being that I dared to have an opinion, I was also dubbed "loud-mouthed fatso." It doesn't have to be clever to be cruel. Not only was I overweight, but I lived in a trailer park. And my family was on welfare. Consequently, I earned additional labels like lazy and stupid. My daddy lost his job when his plant moved to Mexico. Mama worked in a bakery that was attached to a liquor store. Food items were free. You try planning a menu for five children with food from a bakery and a liquor store.

But it wasn't an issue for long because Wal-Mart moved in across the street, forcing the bakery to close down. My brother thought he'd help out by joining the Marines. He was killed in Afghanistan. By friendly fire. You might say my family was living the American nightmare. I developed quite an opinion about the system in which we live. But no one cared about my opinion. Then I saw that Miss Burnet, Texas, was going to speak at fifty-six public engagements during her reign. I realized that the pageantry was the only accessible venue for me to nurture my voice. All I had to do was lose the weight.

It was truly amazing. In one year I went from being a loud-mouth fatso to a well-spoken beauty — without changing one single word. As a beauty candidate I made over two thousand public appearances. No one tired of the Kayla-the-Whale-a story. In my travels, I was astounded by the number of people who had their own tales of childhood labels. Yet no one ever bragged about being a bully. How could this be? We can't all be victims.

Then I remembered my own young attempts at retaliation. I used to call evil Monica Snyder "Treasure" on account of her sunken chest. Today, that woman is probably paying a plastic surgeon for her new, super-sized enhancements. My motivational program, "Freeing the Fatso Within," has nothing to do with losing weight. It's about realizing that we are all simply running from our childhood labels. No matter how much weight I lose, I will always be Kayla the Whale-a. When I won the junior high science fair, everyone attacked my appearance. When I became a beauty queen, they crucified my mind. Consequently, I learned that labels are the fuel of empowerment. How else could a fat, lazy, stupid, sucking-the-system-dry, trailer-park-trash kid amount to anything? Daddy used to call my sister and me his dream girls. I'd say that this label is the one that best describes the woman I am today.

Better Places to Go
by David-Matthew Barnes

This imaginative monologue introduces the indomitable Rosie, a hard-nosed, embittered waitress in her early twenties, who works at a roadside diner in rural Nebraska and regrets that she has nowhere else to go. Her initial demeanor is intense and unsettling with an exaggerated sense of urgency and seriousness. In a moment of seemingly charming grace, however, Rosie confides in a coworker her "secret" to earning big tips from unsuspecting customers. Her confession is a fanciful, lighthearted, and zestfully comic charade that reaches a climactic frenzy of remorse and regret before descending into darkness.

ROSIE: People like me. They give me tips. *(Beat)* It's part of the job. I tell people what they want to hear. I pretend to be someone that I'm not just to make them happy. It makes people feel better about themselves if they think they're helping someone who is *less* than them. Like they're doing some good deed for the white trash of the world. Idiots don't realize I'm smarter than them. I get them their drinks. I bring them plates of food. I tell the wives they look young and I flirt with the husbands. I touch their ugly babies, pat their heads, kiss their sticky faces. It's their money that I really want. They always leave me a little extra, because I'm so sweet. *(She pretends, very convincingly, that she is waiting on a customer.)* What a beautiful family you have. It's always nice to see people so happy together. Really, it warms my heart. *(The façade is gone.)* I know how to get what I want. *(Beat)* Yeah, I got big plans tonight. You just don't know, Ricardo. I'm so sick and tired of this place. I'd love to set it on fire and watch it burn to the ground. *(Beat)* You got any matches on you? It gets to a person after a while. It crawls all over me like a rash. Like poison ivy. *(Beat)* How in hell did I get stuck in *Nebraska?*

CHAPTER 7
SCENE STUDY

"Calm down! Only your whole career depends on this scene."
— Alfred Hitchcock, *The Dark Side of Genius*

The following scenes are presented to encourage a relaxed and natural approach to scene study and performance in a classroom setting. The scenes should also promote a more personal, individual character interpretation because they are based upon contemporary flesh-and-blood role models and mirror characters drawn from common walks of life. These contemporary scenes are also more firmly rooted in the "here and now," so any performance approach should be more restrained and subtle than role-playing on a traditional stage.

There are moments of genuine humor and gentle frivolity that suggest the bonds of compassion and mutual understanding between characters, and there are moments of grim reality that recall childhood memories, adolescent scars, or frustrated wishful dreams that were never realized. The characters exhibit courage and conviction even while engaging in innocent blunders, displaying outrageous behavior, committing errors in judgment, or simply displaying basic human urges such as anger, fear, frustration, or despair.

The challenge in playing these selected scenes is to act instinctively and to make daring performance choices that build moment-to-moment anticipation and suspense that is only resolved at the climactic resolution of the episode. Remember that these contemporary scenes feature stage figures that are very much "like us today." So search for appropriate bodily actions, gestures, and movement that reinforce the character portraits, and chart believable character vocal and physical changes that give your portraits distinction and dimension.

As part of your initial preparation for classroom performance, focus on the "tempo" that underscores the attitude or mood of the characters for the most immediate and meaningful impact, and assume a performance attitude that suggests the roles are being played for the first time and in the present moment. Remember that some of the scenes feature more than two characters, so look for acting partners capable of capturing incisive character portraits that are truly memorable and individual in nuance.

Role-Playing

In playing these contemporary roles in a classroom setting, it is important that the performance style be more restrained or subtle in both voice and body. This approach to classroom performance should promote a more personal, individual character portrait that has believability and integrity because it is based upon a real-life model. It may be useful to integrate appropriate personal traits and mannerisms that help to reinforce your character portrait and to chart vocal and physical changes that will permit you to "visualize" how the character will look and sound to the audience.

Finally, in playing contemporary scenes, it is important to pay careful attention to surface details and minor character flaws as potential clues for interpretation and performance. This illustrative approach to character building — giving a personal life and meaning to the given circumstances, images, or objects associated with the character — can be an invaluable ingredient in your classroom performance as well. Remember to keep in mind that an honest, believable character portrait is one that any spectator could easily recognize and just as easily identify in his or her own similar life experiences.

Le Supermache
by Ian August

This clever and charming fable about true love, winner of the 31st annual Samuel French, Inc. Off-Off Broadway Short Play Festival, is a deliciously fractured fairy tale in food-speak and all things culinary. It starts with a precocious Girl and then adds a heroic Boy. They innocently meet in the magical aisles of Le Supermarche amid the glossy labels and glistening produce, fall instantly in love, marry, and move to a quaint cottage in the country. The blissful romance soon sours, however, when the Girl begins to curdle in her milquetoast life and flees back to the market to find solace and peace. Instead, she encounters a mysterious figure who offers her a delicious but dangerous recipe to cure her marital woes. What follows is a romantic romp wrapped in wit and satire but spiced with a dose of frosty revenge.

(The set is that of a kitchen interior. One non-moving countertop with stove lies Stage Center. Behind the counter rests kitchen cabinets, from which the actors will remove props and scene pieces. There is a refrigerator façade beside the cabinets, from which the Boy will make all entrances and exits. The countertop acts as an all-purpose set piece for chairs, the bed, stove, etc. Lights up on the Narrator Stage Center. Behind him on either side, frozen in athletic tableau, are the Boy, in chef's hat, and the Girl, in apron. As he speaks, they come to life.)

NARRATOR: "Le Supermarche" or "What I Did for Lunch." The characters: the Girl —

GIRL: A Girl.

NARRATOR: The Boy —

BOY: A Boy.

NARRATOR: The setting: somewhere that is not France. The time: sometime that is not too long ago. *(Beat)* It starts with a Girl.

GIRL: Hello.

NARRATOR: And then adds a Boy.

BOY: How ya doin?

NARRATOR: Basic recipes require basic ingredients. *(To GIRL)* On the one side: chewy, slender, sinuous; perfect for stocks and sauces. Bring the pot to a boil; add carrots, celery, fennel, two small red onions and a three-inch-long piece of ginger root.

GIRL: I adore ginger root.

NARRATOR: Salt and pepper to taste. For the more adventurous palate, try a little sweet basil for that something extra.

GIRL: I used to have a smoky flavor, but then I tried the patch.

NARRATOR: *(To BOY)* And on the other side: bold, broad, hefty and savory — whether the heart of the stew or the filling of the crepe. Juicy, bloody and tenderized barely within the boundaries of decency — nearly falling off the bone.

BOY: I'm leaner than I used to be.

NARRATOR: And we love you all the more for it.

GIRL: I know I do.

NARRATOR: They meet in le supermarche.

BOY: We're French?

NARRATOR: Le supermarche, where silver-wrapped confections play hide-and-seek behind picket fenced registers; where clean-ups abound in aisle five, home of boxed soups, salad dressings, cooking oils and condiments of assorted viscous quality; where swift bursts of spray make tiered produce glisten in the halo of fluorescent light above.

BOY and GIRL: It's beautiful.

NARRATOR: It starts. Reaching for the same bruised head of radicchio.

BOY: I'm sorry ... my fault.

GIRL: No, it's mine.

NARRATOR: There is an instantaneous connection.

BOY: I've seen you here before.

GIRL: I've been here many times.

BOY: So have I.

GIRL: You have? *(Pause)* I'm twenty-three years old and I don't expect to live past thirty. I recently moved out of my parent's house into a really cozy studio uptown where the landlady calls me "hon" and my next door neighbor has three cats named Blinky, Slinky, and Melba. I'm a Sagittarius and passionate about my art and my work and my family and my manicures. Do these avocados look ripe to you? You can stop me any time and tell me that you love me.

BOY: And I do.

NARRATOR: And they do. A whirlwind romance, coupled with a burning infatuation for all things delicious. Observe.

GIRL: Tell me how you love me.

BOY: I love you the way custard grows in beige flowers on a bed of lime gelato.

GIRL: Yes?

BOY: I love you the way crystal shimmers in the light bouncing through shitake consommé.

GIRL: Yes?

BOY: I love you the way Jarlsburg Swiss lays languorous over a *hot-heavy-open-faced Reuben. (Pause)*

GIRL: You have a lovely way with words. *(They kiss hungrily.)*

NARRATOR: The scene is stirred, and liberally sweetened with Splenda. And as the watched pot comes to a boil, the Girl and the Boy are married. They move to a little house in the country where he garnishes her with gourmet gifts and she services him with succulent snackings. But like all vegetables who sit in the sun too long, the Girl begins to wilt beneath the brilliant light of his love. *(BOY leaves into fridge.)*

GIRL: At night I cry with tears that are salty like beef jerky. I love my husband. I love his touch and his taste, but I miss the pleasures of my youth: my simple past, my studio apartment and the landlady who called me "hon," and Blinky and Slinky and Melba. I miss my art and my work and my family and my manicures. And how can I possibly die at age thirty? *(He enters from fridge.)*

BOY: Syrup, I'm home. How was your morning?

GIRL: Bland.

BOY: And your afternoon?

GIRL: Tepid.

BOY: I sent you flowers at lunch — did you get them?

GIRL: I ate them.

BOY: Walnut, what's going on? We were so happy before. What can I do to make your pain evaporate? My heart is heavy with cream.

NARRATOR: She does not answer, for what can she say? So she stews.

GIRL: I simmer.

NARRATOR: She blanches.

GIRL: I boil.

NARRATOR: She fries.

GIRL: I bake.

NARRATOR: It's healthier. Remove from the oven at 350 degrees and poke the top with a toothpick. If it's done, the toothpick will emerge clean as a whistle. *(The BOY pokes her with a toothpick; she turns on him.)*

GIRL: *(Angrily)* It's clean. I'm done. *(BOY exits into fridge.)*

NARRATOR: So she returns to the place of her comfort, the place of her peace, the place where walls are lined with brightly colored cans of beans and aisles are draped with banners saying, "Buy,

Buy!" and "50 Cents Off Two Bags of Muffins!"

GIRL: Le supermarche.

NARRATOR: And it is here, wandering among the frozen fish patties, where she meets — the Shrink-Wrapped Man. *(The NARRATOR becomes the SHRINK-WRAPPED MAN.)*

GIRL: Who ... are you?

SHRINK-WRAPPED MAN: I come when saline stains the tiles
To offer aid and send for smiles
For when the kugel hits the fan
They call for me — the Shrink-Wrapped Man.

GIRL: You speak in couplets.

SHRINK-WRAPPED MAN: Why so glum, my little peach?
With happiness so near your reach?

GIRL: Do I have to respond in couplets?

SHRINK-WRAPPED MAN: Allow me to endear myself
Before I jump back on the shelf
I sense in you a great unrest
That lies beneath your turkey breast.

GIRL: You're right. You're strange, but you're right. I'm flustered. I'm frustrated. I feel eclaired and ignored. I hate my life, and I hate our little house, and I'm so furious with my husband I could scream —

SHRINK-WRAPPED MAN: But ere you share your noise pollution
I have for you a quick solution:
(The SHRINK-WRAPPED MAN hands her a package.)
Within this packet you desire
Resides ingredients of fire
Create concoctions piping hot
A sumptuous stew to hit the spot
Just sprinkle chili with this spice —
I'm sure your spouse will not think twice
For even with one tiny taste,
Your sour will turn sweet — post-haste!

GIRL: Wait, I'm confused. My life will improve if I feed this to my hubby?

SHRINK-WRAPPED MAN: Just take my missive by the letter
And what was vile will taste much better!

GIRL: You're very impressive. You should write a book.

(The SHRINK-WRAPPED MAN becomes the NARRATOR.)
NARRATOR: And with that, the Shrink-Wrapped Man was gone.
GIRL: Where'd he go? *(BOY re-enters from the fridge; he and GIRL lie in bed.)*
NARRATOR: That night, beneath a crescent moon —
BOY: *(Correcting him)* Croissant moon. We're French, remember?
NARRATOR: While her husband slept, his wife lay beside him — like salad, tossing, and like rotisserie chicken, turning — the words of the Shrink-Wrapped Man echoing in her head. And when the cinnamon morning rolled around she had slept barely a wink.
BOY: Baby Greens, you're so tired. I can see it in your eyes.
GIRL: *(Curtly)* I think it's something I ate.
BOY: Why don't I come home early today? We'll have lunch and spend the rest of the day loafing together. Does that sound nice? Sweet potato? Ratatouille?
GIRL: I'll make lunch. A chili. Meaty and strong and spicy.
BOY: Sounds amazing. I'll be home at noon. *(He kisses her on the cheek, exits. The GIRL grabs a pan from a cabinet.)*
NARRATOR: In a medium-size saucepan she warms over the stove, her oil begins to sizzle, her garlic begins to pop. And the morning passes as molasses.
GIRL: Nine-thirty. Ten-seventeen. Eleven o'clock.
NARRATOR: *(With sinister glee)* And now, placing herself over high heat, the Girl begins to mix the mysterious chili. In a Calphalon Commercial Nonstick 10-inch Everyday Pan with Lid, she adds: one pound ground beef; one can kidney beans, drained; half of a Vidalia onion and half of a green bell pepper, seeded, stemmed, washed and chilled. Then she reaches for the packet from the strange old man.
GIRL: After all, revenge is a dish best served with dried pepper flakes.
NARRATOR: And it starts.
GIRL: *(Á la the witches of* Macbeth*)* This bag of spice to do the chore
Ingredients with heat galore:
A bit of chili powder here,
A tiny drop of Worcestershire,
And in the pot that he's consumin'
A modest healthy dose of cumin.

159

A jalapeno, mustard seed
And horseradish to suit the need.
One habanero, hint of sage,
Two parts Tabasco — one part *rage!*
(There is an explosion from her pan.)

BOY: *(Re-entering from the refrigerator with a bouquet of broccoli.)* Salmon, I brought these for you.

GIRL: Put them in the crisper with the others. You hungry?

BOY: Famished! Mmmmm. It smells incredible!

GIRL: Have some. *(She dishes him some chili.)* Bon appetit!

BOY: *(Turning to an audience member, aside)* We're French. *(The BOY looks up at the GIRL, grabs a spoon, and takes a mouthful of the chili. His eyes open widely.)*

NARRATOR: The Girl looks on anxiously as the Boy takes a spoonful of the mixture. She can see the tears welling up in his eyes; his face becomes lobster red; she can feel the heat radiating from his body. And she thinks:

GIRL: This is it! He'll finally understand my unhappiness! The chili must be totally *inedible*.

NARRATOR: But the Boy simply looks at her and smiles.

BOY: *(With some difficulty.)* It's delicious.

NARRATOR: And with sweat streaming down his tomato face, he takes another bite.

GIRL: What?

NARRATOR: And another.

GIRL: No —

NARRATOR: And another.

GIRL: Stop!

NARRATOR: But he does not stop. The Girl stands helpless as bite after bite, spoonful after spoonful, the chili in front of her husband begins to disappear. In pain, impassioned and determined, the Boy licks the Corningware clean.

GIRL: He can't —

NARRATOR: But he did. Look.

GIRL: *(To the BOY)* But why, Corn Chip? Why would you keep eating?

NARRATOR: The Boy opened his mouth, but no words could come.

For having consumed the entire bowl of chili, it had rendered him unable to speak. And more terrible yet — it had left him completely bereft of the ability to taste.

GIRL: What were you thinking?

NARRATOR: And looking up into her eyes, the Boy wished that he could tell her — wished that he could share with her —

BOY: *(To NARRATOR)* Uh, excuse me — d'you mind if I take this one?

NARRATOR: Not at all. Looking up into her eyes, but unable to speak, the Boy delivers a silent monologue.

BOY: *(To GIRL)* Oh, Sno-cone, I know you're unhappy. I know you've given up everything to be with me. And with every red-hot bite I could feel your anger, and I could taste your pain. But I couldn't stop. I had to go on. Because you made it for me. You chopped for me, you diced for me, you simmered for me and you spiced for me. And underneath that volcanic rage is a love that I know still warms your heart, as your chili warms my stomach. Within that chili was the heart of you. I've lost my ability to speak and I've lost my ability to taste, but I will never lose my ability to love you.

GIRL: Oh, that's beautiful.

BOY: I wish you could have heard it.

GIRL: Me, too. *(There is a pause, and the GIRL goes to the pan.)*

NARRATOR: And before you can say "Blackened Scrod with Bok Choy Wrapped Couscous and Grilled Eggplant Sandwiches," the Girl takes up the spoon and begins eating the remains of the poisonous chili, right out of the pan! Her eyes burn and her hair sizzles, and when she is done, she, too, is left without speech, without taste, but with a fire burning in her heart hotter than it ever had before.

GIRL: Don't I get a monologue?

NARRATOR: No. In their anguish, in their passion, the Boy and the Girl find a true love once more: a love greater than a fifty-pound bag of potatoes, a love stronger than a well-aged slab of gorgonzola, a love gentler than the aroma from a freshly snipped sprig of dill. A love not unlike the most scrumptious concoctions. But before the recipe can be perfected, tidbits have to burn, temperatures regulated, conditions adjusted. Isn't that the way of all great meals? *(The BOY and the GIRL nod vigorously, turn to each other, and freeze in an athletic tableau.)*

NARRATOR: And together they lived for the rest of their days, happily united by a mute but mutual understanding of one another, a newly developed appreciation for texture, and the praline and cream memory of their first culinary encounter — over a bruised head of radicchio — in Le Supermarche.

Decisions, Decisions
by Ken Friedman

This hilarious duo scene is an antic blend of high-spirited and sparkling humor that features a flamboyant but insecure young male actor rehearsing for his "first big break" in a professional production and his ferociously loyal female friend, who is determined that her friend will ultimately succeed. Bert, an inexperienced but enthusiastic actor, has just been cast in his first New York role and is furiously rehearsing his role with Karen, a carefree friend who has volunteered to be his rehearsal partner. The rehearsal period is memorable in its exaggerated blend of acting vigor and yet rich in its artful ingenuity and inventiveness. The fun bubbles along right through a smashing climax and is a nonstop roller coaster hymn of theatrical clichés and rehearsal missteps that can be both funny and painful at the same time.

(Two actors in rehearsal anywhere.)
KAREN: It's a great opportunity; grab it.
BERT: But, Karen, I don't know if it's the right one.
KAREN: Bert, for God's sakes, your first role in New York after three years. Grab it and make it work.
BERT: Right. You're right. Thank you.
KAREN: I mean, are you nude? Do you eat body parts? What?
BERT: Well, first of all, it's a play about the Korean War.
KAREN: The what war?
BERT: Korean.
KAREN: Drama or comedy?
BERT: Drama.

KAREN: The Korean War? Is it fictional?

BERT: No, there actually was one.

KAREN: Really? I never heard of it.

BERT: See?

KAREN: That doesn't mean anything. It could be one of those quiet wars with a large cult following. Who was in it?

BERT: Us and Korea. China and maybe Ireland. I couldn't tell.

KAREN: OK. Reputable countries. So, what is your problem?

BERT: Well, who's going to come and see it?

KAREN: No one. It's a showcase. Have you read the script?

BERT: Twice.

KAREN: Good?

BERT: I have no idea. I asked the director what it meant.

KAREN: Before you read it, or after you read it?

BERT: Before. I didn't want to read it and still not know.

KAREN: Smart. Very professional. And he said?

BERT: He's not quite sure, but he thinks it's a metaphor.

KAREN: I like that. I respect any director that can turn what he doesn't understand into a metaphor. I think a heartfelt vagueness is essential to the success of any play. Are you a soldier?

BERT: Yes. I open the show.

KAREN: Fantastic.

BERT: With three lines.

KAREN: To open the show? Good. Very Good.

BERT: No, I have three lines for the entire show. The curtain rises. I'm in a foxhole. I stand and shout: "Look! An eagle! A free bird in flight. How I envy your proud plumage!" That's it.

KAREN: That's a very nice speech.

BERT: And *bang!* I get it. A sniper. Off-stage. And after that I lie there. Dead. That's it. I'm dead.

KAREN: For how long do you lie there or is it lay?

BERT: Either way, two hours. No intermission. Two hours of my back to the audience. The director doesn't want them to see my face, because my nose could twitch. So I ask, Karen … do you think that this is the New York debut that will advance my career?

KAREN: Bert, are you crazy? A lot of actors would kill for that role. Do the lines. I want to hear. Do them. Do them. Please. *(He reveals* *a huge script.)*

BERT: Performance level? From beginning to end?

KAREN: Yes. Let's find out what they mean. *(He prepares.)*

BERT: OK … I'm not really sure yet. But, here goes … *(He lies down, gets up.)* Wait! Help me. Be the eagle. Fly. Fly like an eagle.

KAREN: Good idea. Focus on me. I'm on my perch. Here I go! I'm flying. Do eagles make sounds?

BERT: If they want to, sure.

KAREN: *(She flies around.)* Coooo … Coooo. Watch the birdie.

BERT: No, no. You're flying like a parakeet. Be grand. Big wings. Swoop. Soar. Better. Much better. Yes!

KAREN: Ready? Here I come. The form, the face of a hunter. *(She is flying. He jumps to his feet.)*

BERT: Look! An eagle! A free bird in flight. How I envy your proud plumage!

KAREN: Gunshot!

BERT: Bang. Aghhhh … aghhhh … *(He twists and as he is falling …)*

KAREN: Ohhhh! *(She is also falling.)*

BERT: *Ma! I'm dying!* I love you … Maaaa. Ohhhh. *(He hits the floor as KAREN lands on top of him. They get up together.)* Well?

KAREN: Wow! You must do the part! You were so real.

BERT: Thank you. Did you like the ad-lib? About my mother? I had to do it. But, what were you doing? It was my scene and you landed on me.

KAREN: He shot me, too. I couldn't help it. I was so into it. But, you were communicating so much of … you know, death, pain, grief. All that stuff.

BERT: I feel it. I wasn't sure, but now I know. I'm an actor. And I must act.

KAREN: No question about it. You can do this. It may be three lines, but on your resume, it'll look like a lead.

BERT: Thank you, Karen. I needed to hear that. Now, this brings me to my next question.

KAREN: What? What else is there?

BERT: Should I invite agents?

KAREN: Absolutely. They leave at intermission anyway. Bert, you haven't mentioned my eagle.

BERT: Very good. Very helpful. You had a real sense of bird.

KAREN: Thank you. And call your parents and let them know.

BERT: I'll have to write. They just got an unlisted number. Then it's settled. I'm going to do it. My first play in New York. It may not be much, but after my lines, I'll get plenty of much-needed rest. I just hope I don't fall asleep.

KAREN: And, you don't know. In this business, you never know.

BERT: It could lead to something. Come on, let's get out of here and go rent a movie. Look, look — an eagle in flight. I'll take the script. I may want to make some changes. *(They hurriedly exit.)*

Yellow Brick Road
by Paula Stone

This magical and original retelling of the C. Frank Baum classic fantasy may not feature the beloved Munchkins, Scarecrow, Tin Woodman, or even the Wizard of Oz, but it is cleverly constructed, full of artful ingenuity and a snappy satire. Here we see a confident and headstrong Dorothy and a mature, star-struck Auntie Em both in a wickedly amusing quest for the lure of Hollywood stardust. The scene is the rundown Kansas farm that Dorothy has returned to after her star turn in the film and her decision to move to Hollywood that sets in motion a train of events that leads a panic-stricken and desperate Auntie Em to also fall under the alluring spell of cinema magic. From this point on, it's a tug of war for the ruby red slippers!

AUNTIE EM: Oh, Dorothy, I was so afraid I was never going to see you again.

DOROTHY: If only you could have been there, Auntie Em. It was so beautiful.

AUNTIE EM: Never mind, dear. You're home again and that's all that matters. Now lie down and rest and I'll get you a nice mug of hot milk and some of your favorite cookies.

DOROTHY: Auntie Em — please don't treat me like a little girl. My future is at stake.

AUNTIE EM: Of course it is, dear. But your future is here with me.

DOROTHY: Please, Auntie Em. I want to go back to Hollywood.

AUNTIE EM: But I'm getting old now, and I need you here.

DOROTHY: But I want to become a star.

AUNTIE EM: I don't think so, Dorothy. Besides, you love Kansas and helping here on the farm. What would I do without you?

DOROTHY: Kansas! But where's that? Not when there's a big, wide, wonderful world out there, full of yellow brick roads and munchkins and glittering emerald cities.

AUNTIE EM: That may be true, dear. But there are also wicked witches and lying lizards out there. No — that world is too dangerous for you.

DOROTHY: Oh pooh, Auntie Em. You don't have to worry. I'll be safe, as long as I have my ruby slippers with me.

AUNTIE EM: I said no. I mean, what if something happens to me? Who will take care of me? Who will take care of the farm?

DOROTHY: Uncle Henry will, or Hunk or Zeke or Hickory — Anyway, you're as fit as a fiddle. Never been sick a day in your life. You'll be just fine.

AUNTIE EM: But I've been counting on you, Dorothy.

DOROTHY: And you still can, Auntie. I'll come back to visit you — I promise — every Christmas.

AUNTIE EM: That's not good enough.

DOROTHY: Oh, Auntie Em — you've been like a mother to me, and I'm very grateful, honest, and I love you. But I have my own life to live now.

AUNTIE EM: Young lady — you are not going anywhere. This is where you belong, here, with me.

DOROTHY: Well, maybe you belong on a farm — wearing the same old apron every day, feeding chickens, slaving over a hot stove —

AUNTIE EM: What? Wait a minute. Something's the matter with my apron?

DOROTHY: It's a lovely apron. It's just that, in Hollywood, every day I can wear pretty dresses and rouge and let my hair flow free.

AUNTIE EM: My bun? Hair? Free?

DOROTHY: I've made up my mind, Auntie, and now I'm going to start packing — Oh, no! Auntie Em! What's the matter? You OK?

AUNTIE EM: Yes. Fine. Just a bit dizzy. Never mind me.

DOROTHY: Here. Sit. Let me help you.

AUNTIE EM: No — please — stay away from me.

DOROTHY: But I've never seen you so pale. I'll run and get Uncle Henry.

AUNTIE EM: *No* — leave him be. He's busy cleaning out the pig pen.

DOROTHY: Then the doctor? Should I call the doctor? Auntie, do you want me to call the doctor?

AUNTIE EM: What I want is for you to get out of here quick —

DOROTHY: Oh golly gee —

AUNTIE EM: — While you still have the chance.

DOROTHY: But Auntie Em!

AUNTIE EM: Now go!

DOROTHY: But I can't leave you like this! How can I?

AUNTIE EM: Well then — maybe you won't have to — Give me those ruby slippers. *(AUNTIE EM grabs the ruby slippers and starts to put them on.)* I had dreams for my life too, you know. And they didn't include being stuck on a godforsaken farm someplace in the middle of nowhere being tossed around by tornadoes. Maybe your being in that movie was a good thing after all. I'm leaving with you, kiddo. *(AUNTIE EM grabs the suitcase, shuts her eyes, and clicks the heels of the ruby slippers.)* There's no place like Hollywood. There's no place like Hollywood. There's no place like Hollywood.

Anger Management
by Lindsay Price

In this warmly delightful, satiric spoof of two of William Shakespeare's most celebrated tragic heroines, Juliet and Ophelia meet in a psychiatrist's waiting room in the afterworld for an anger management appointment. Surrounded by an air of mystery and menace, this seemingly light-hearted reunion turns quickly into a breath-stopping and farcical exorcism of the anger, guilt, and regret that has plagued each of the heroines throughout the years of their untimely deaths. A cleverly conceived, keenly observant, and often very funny examination of the frustration and hostility Juliet and Ophelia are experiencing follows under the most unexpected circumstances. In a nonstop cavalcade of comic wit and mayhem, with an underlying literary glow, Juliet and Ophelia relive their disturbing destiny for which, sadly, William Shakespeare's disjointed times had condemned them.

(JULIET sits in a psychiatrist's waiting room. She has a puzzled look on her face as she tries to figure out a Yoga for Dummies *book.)*

JULIET: *(Reading)* The shoulder stand. One of the best poses for relaxation and meditation. Huh. *(She turns the book around.)* That does not look relaxing. That looks like the farthest thing from relaxing. *(Tosses book.)* Stupid book. *(OPHELIA enters. She sighs as she slumps into one of the chairs.)*

JULIET: Hey.

OPHELIA: Hello. *(She sighs again.)*

JULIET: Are you OK?

OPHELIA: Sorry. Sorry, I'm not — I don't like this.

JULIET: This … chair?

OPHELIA: Dr. Jodi.

JULIET: Gotcha.

OPHELIA: I hate it. And her. Sorry.

JULIET: Don't be. She's very annoying.

OPHELIA: *(Perking up)* You don't like her?

JULIET: *(Sing-song)* Hate her.

OPHELIA: *(A little happier)* Really?

JULIET: Since the very beginning.

OPHELIA: *(Really happy)* Really?

JULIET: I hate that it's Dr. Jodi. Not just Jodi, and not Dr. Chung —

BOTH: Dr. Jodi.

OPHELIA: I thought everybody around here liked her.

JULIET: You'd think she's cured cancer the way they talk about her in the commissary.

OPHELIA: I know. *(Mocking)* She's the best. She's so helpful.

JULIET: *(Mocking)* She got me to open right up. Opened right up like a flower.

OPHELIA: I hate that one. That one and — I'd go to Dr. Jodi even if

168

I didn't have to.

JULIET: I hate that! I hate that we have to go.

OPHELIA: Try telling her.

JULIET: Oh, I have. Didn't go over so well. *(A little too loud)* I'm missing the point of Dr. Jodi. *(Whispers.)* Apparently.

OPHELIA: We haven't met. Have we? No.

JULIET: Not officially. I've seen you around.

OPHELIA: That must be it.

JULIET: I've seen you in the commissary.

OPHELIA: We're always around.

JULIET: We don't have very many places to go.

OPHELIA: You've been around a long time.

JULIET: Uh huh. You too.

OPHELIA: I can't believe we haven't met. Officially.

JULIET: I don't really socialize.

OPHELIA: Right. Me either.

JULIET: People come and go.

OPHELIA: They're mostly here and then they're gone.

JULIET: Yeah. They're mostly annoying too.

OPHELIA: Yeah. Mostly. Almost all.

JULIET: Makes you want to claw your eyes out.

OPHELIA: Yeah. Have you been seeing Dr. Jodi long?

JULIET: Seems like.

OPHELIA: Long time.

JULIET: Centuries even.

OPHELIA: Seems like. Sorry — *(Sticking her hand out)* I'm Ophelia.

JULIET: Juliet. Juliet Capulet. *(They shake hands.)*

OPHELIA: Nice to meet you.

JULIET: Officially.

OPHELIA: Right. *(Pause)* So. Did you … *(Gestures vaguely.)*

JULIET: Oh, yes.

OPHELIA: Me, too.

JULIET: Really?

OPHELIA: That's how we got the golden ticket to Loserville.

JULIET: I guess. How did you … *(Gestures vaguely.)*

OPHELIA: Drowned myself.

JULIET: *(Pointing at herself)* Knife in the stomach.

OPHELIA: Ow! Really?

JULIET: It's all … foggy.

OPHELIA: Yeah! It went totally foggy for me. I went mad beforehand.

JULIET: Really?

OPHELIA: One second I was in the east hall, the next I'm underwater. Surprise!

JULIET: You're not mad now.

OPHELIA: No, no. I see everything clear as a bell. *(She starts tapping her foot.)* I see a lot of things clear as day. *(The foot tapping gets faster.)* A lot of things, a lot, a … *(She takes a deep breath.)* Sorry. Dr. Jodi says I have anger issues.

JULIET: Me, too.

OPHELIA: Really?

JULIET: Anger management program.

OPHELIA: Me, too! I think I have a lot to be angry about.

JULIET: Being dead makes me angry.

OPHELIA: I hate being dead!

JULIET: It sucks.

OPHELIA: It sucks being dead.

JULIET: Dr. Jodi wouldn't like that kind of talk.

OPHELIA: Tell me about it.

JULIET: Now, now, Juliet. Now, now.

OPHELIA: Now Ophelia, wouldn't you like to find peace?

JULIET: Where will those kind of feelings get you?

OPHELIA: Sometimes, I want to shove her glasses up her nose.

JULIET: Sometimes, I want to shove that bobble head up her nose. The one on her desk?

OPHELIA: She changes them, have you noticed?

JULIET: It's the mood of the day. The mood of the day bobble head.

OPHELIA: I would totally feel so much better if I shoved a bobble head up her nose.

JULIET: It would be awesome!

OPHELIA: Guess my mood, Dr. Jodi!

JULIET: Up yours, Dr. Jodi! Up yours! *(They are now standing and quite loud. They look around to see if someone heard them. They sit slowly.)*

OPHELIA: *(Whispering)* She keeps pushing the crafts on me. I'm supposed to find them calming.

JULIET: *(Whispering)* She says I have to do yoga.

OPHELIA: Do you like it?

JULIET: Hate it. Do you like the crafts?

OPHELIA: I hate the crafts.

JULIET: They're stupid crafts! Why do we have to make birdhouses and Popsicle stick picture frames? Are there any birds?

OPHELIA: None.

JULIET: None! No birds. We're building empty birdhouses for eternity for nothing! We're making frame after empty Popsicle stick frame with no pictures to fill them.

OPHELIA: I got assigned extra Dr. Jodi time because I questioned the sanity of decorative macramé pot holders. There are no pots. Why do we need pot holders, decorative or otherwise? I have nowhere to decorate, no one to decorate for, and as far as I'm concerned, the epitome of uselessness is the decorative pot holder.

JULIET: I hate Thursday afternoon cake.

OPHELIA: It's never good cake.

JULIET: The frosting is disgusting.

OPHELIA: And the way they write *Thursday* on the top. 'Cause none of us have birthdays or anniversaries. That's the only thing to celebrate. *Thursday.*

JULIET: I hate the bingo, I hate the shuffleboard —

OPHELIA: I can live with shuffleboard. *(Hypnotic)* There's something about the way the puck swooshes across the floor. Drifting, drifting. It's peaceful. Mesmerizing. Swooosh. *(Changing tone)* But then I remember what happened and I get angry all over again.

JULIET: You can't let go of the past.

OPHELIA: I hold the past in an iron fist.

JULIET: A death grip.

OPHELIA: A post-death grip.

JULIET: Ha!

OPHELIA: Dr. Jodi give you the "let go of the past" speech?

JULIET: If you want to … move on … Juliet, you need to be calmer. More peaceful.

OPHELIA: Just like the shuffleboard, Ophelia. Calm and peaceful.

JULIET: You need to let go …
OPHELIA: Swooosh.
JULIET: Let go of the past, Juliet …
OPHELIA: Hmmmm. Maybe I hate shuffleboard.
JULIET: The past is the past and it's past.
OPHELIA: The past is done.
JULIET: Now you see the past, now you don't.
OPHELIA: The past is so last year.
JULIET: I don't want to let go of my past. I like getting angry when I think about my past.
OPHELIA: Being angry makes me feel good.
JULIET: It makes me alive.
OPHELIA: Were you allowed to get angry when you were alive?
JULIET: Never.
OPHELIA: Me neither. I want to relive the past over and over again so I can get really angry about it. I love feeling angry!
JULIET: Stupid Romeo!
OPHELIA: Stupid Hamlet!
JULIET: Did you go mad over a guy?
OPHELIA: I got a two-fer. There was a guy *and* I was being manipulated by my dad.
JULIET: You too?
OPHELIA: Really?
JULIET: My dad said I had to marry a guy I totally didn't want to marry, and when I said I wouldn't marry him 'cause I'd already married someone else, he freaked out!
OPHELIA: No!
JULIET: What is it with parents?
OPHELIA: My guy told me to get lost, my dad died, and the next thing I know … did you do it over your dad?
JULIET: A guy. A guy I knew for one day. How could I have been so stupid?
OPHELIA: Where's he? Did he … *(Gestures vaguely.)*
JULIET: Oh, yeah. Poison. Over me. Supposedly he loved me *so* much he couldn't live without me and took poison over my dead body. That is supposedly a big heap of love.
OPHELIA: So he's here?

JULIET: Oh, no. He moved on.

OPHELIA: He left you behind?

JULIET: Oh, yeah. Eons ago. How's that for true love?

OPHELIA: No wonder you're upset. Did you love him?

JULIET: Enough to knife myself in the stomach. Now, not so much.

OPHELIA: What is it with guys? Why are our entire lives ruled by them? I never had one single solitary thought to myself when I was alive. Not one. Go here, Ophelia. Do this, Ophelia. Let me tell you what you're thinking, Ophelia. To a nunnery, Ophelia!

JULIET: Oh, I thought for myself. Thought for myself right into a knife in the stomach.

OPHELIA: If I had just had a single solitary thought, I wouldn't have ended up in that river. I know it.

JULIET: You were insane. You could hardly help it.

OPHELIA: What's the deal with going insane for a guy? Guys suck!

JULIET: Romeo picks his nose!

OPHELIA: Hamlet farts and walks away!

JULIET: Romeo wears socks and sandals!

OPHELIA: Why would I want to move on? I'd just have to be happy about seeing all the people who jerked me around in my life. Do I really want to see them all that much?

JULIET: It's not that bad here. No parents telling you to marry some dope who has hairy monkey breath.

OPHELIA: Exactly! Why would I want to move on? *(Standing)* Come on!

JULIET: Where are we going?

OPHELIA: To yell at Dr. Jodi! We're going to stay angry for the rest of eternity. Let's celebrate our anger!

JULIET: The commissary has chocolate mint ice cream.

OPHELIA: To anger and chocolate mint ice cream!

JULIET: To anger! Huzzah!

OPHELIA: Huzzah! *(They exit.)*

Attic Letters
by Jeanne Beckwith

Alice and Maureen, two teenage kindred spirits with a keen sense of misadventure, are cleaning out Alice's maternal grandmother's house following Grandma's death when they discover an old box of dusty love letters in the attic. The letters were apparently exchanged over a lifetime by two people who may have gone their separate ways but who continued to share confidences. Frequently charming and funny, what the letters imply — although the two people were physically apart, they were as emotionally close as only true lovers can be — is as revealing as what is actually written down. After reading the letters, the once skeptical Alice and Maureen must now rethink their initial perceptions about true love and old age.

ALICE: Incredible!

MAUREEN: My God! How many are there?

ALICE: Thirty, maybe? At least thirty.

MAUREEN: All that paper!

ALICE: All that ink!

MAUREEN: It must have taken hours to write them.

ALICE: When did he find the time? When did she?

MAUREEN: Why didn't she get rid of them?

ALICE: I don't know. Maybe it was too hard. It wouldn't be like deleting an e-mail. You'd actually have to tear them up one by one — or burn them in a pile. That's a lot of work.

MAUREEN: Maybe she just wanted to hang on to them until the last minute.

ALICE: Why?

MAUREEN: Why? Why do you think? They're hot.

ALICE: Maureen, you are talking about my 89-year old grandmother!

MAUREEN: There is some serious lust going on here. I think it's kinda cool.

ALICE: Cool? My 89-year old grandmother was cool?

MAUREEN: I'd say so. Apparently she was having a love affair up until practically the day she died. I'd say that was pretty cool.

ALICE: It was not very cool to leave all the evidence behind.

MAUREEN: No, but she probably intended to get rid of them and then death sneaked up on her.

ALICE: She was 89! She must have suspected it was a possibility.

MAUREEN: Maybe death always just kind of sneaks up on us.

ALICE: You think she loved this guy?

MAUREEN: He wrote an incredible letter.

ALICE: He did, didn't he?

MAUREEN: Some of these are recent. You think he's still alive?

ALICE: Why? You gonna look him up?

MAUREEN: I might think about it.

ALICE: You're sick.

MAUREEN: Well, your grandmother doesn't need him anymore. I think it's sad to let something like this go to waste.

ALICE: Do you think he was at the funeral?

MAUREEN: There were a lot of geezers there. It could be.

ALICE: "Geezer Lust." Sounds like a song title.

MAUREEN: Well, this old bird could certainly sing. Look at this bit about the porch swing.

ALICE: How could anyone even do it in a porch swing?

MAUREEN: Maybe your grandfather wrote them. He just signs them "Syd." What was your grandfather's name? Would you recognize his handwriting?

ALICE: These are nothing my grandfather ever wrote. I remember my grandfather very well. His name was Martin, and anyway, he would never have — well, he just wouldn't have — not in a porch swing.

MAUREEN: Maybe not, but he's been dead a long time. She's been single since I've known you.

ALICE: She was not single. She was a widow. There's a difference.

MAUREEN: I don't know. Widows have a lot of time on their hands.

ALICE: My mother will crap when she reads these.

MAUREEN: You're going to show them to your mother?

ALICE: Well, I have to, don't I? Technically they're hers.

MAUREEN: You don't have to. Not if it would upset her. Nobody needs an upset mom.

ALICE: Maybe I should just get rid of them

MAUREEN: You should.
ALICE: You're right. I am most definitely getting rid of them.

Dinner for Two
by Ken Friedman

Lois, a seasoned but self-centered young actress with delusions of grandeur, and her low-key, somber friend, Fred, are having dinner at a small café. Lois has a rare gift for staging impromptu "theatrical moments" that are occasionally hilarious but more often than not raucous. Here, she is berating a sullen Fred for his failure to properly acknowledge her recent performance in the production he has just witnessed. Lois seizes the opportunity to introduce Fred to the theatrical ritual of how to address an actor's performance. Her lively lecture on decorum and etiquette is truly remarkable in its indomitable persuasion and self-congratulatory tone that gradually builds in suspense towards an inexorable comic climax.

LOIS: Are you going to pay attention, or aren't you?
FRED: Of course, I'm paying attention.
LOIS: *(To the waiter)* Yes, we're finished. Leave the bread. Thank you.
FRED: *(To the waiter)* Keep the change.
LOIS: Now, to be frank, Fred, my feelings are not hurt.
FRED: How could they be? Lois, I said you were very good. I enjoyed the show. I paid for dinner. What else?
LOIS: You said my performance was great, but that there were a couple of little things —
FRED: Well, there were. But nothing that —
LOIS: Fred, I don't want to strike you in public. In my performance there are never little things. And I don't need to hear about them even if you think there were.
FRED: OK, I'm sorry.
LOIS: I don't want our friendship to suffer, but you simply don't know how to speak to a PPA: Post Performance Actress. It takes skill and some sensitivity.
FRED: I —

LOIS: May I finish? In theatre, there is no such thing as FCC: Friendly Constructive Criticism.

FRED: How was I to know? I'm sorry.

LOIS: All criticism is unfriendly and destructive.

FRED: I meant no harm.

LOIS: So, dump FCC and learn what counts: CCA.

FRED: CCA? What in the world is CCA?

LOIS: Constant Constructive Adoration. This simple and pleasant approach to actors can change your life.

FRED: Really?

LOIS: Sure. So, listen as I teach you the language of Art. Three words: "You were wonderful." And that's it in a nutshell. "You were wonderful." May I hear them please? Now!

FRED: Lois, really.

LOIS: Fred, don't aggravate me. May I hear the words?

FRED: You were wonderful!

LOIS: Again.

FRED: You were wonderful.

LOIS: Disgraceful. Is that the best you can do?

FRED: What do you want from me? Should I play a bugle?

LOIS: Exactly. Put life in to it. Give it guts.

FRED: OK. But this is the last time. You were wonderful.

LOIS: Pathetic. Are you thrilled with me or the tablecloth?

FRED: Well, it's embarrassing. People can hear.

LOIS: *Eureka!* Now, you're catching on. Again. Again.

FRED: You were wonderful.

LOIS: Why are you finding this so difficult?

FRED: You were wonderful. I'm trying. I'm doing my best.

LOIS: Look at me. Hold my hand. And choose one word to emphasize. And the look in your eye? Try awe.

FRED: Lois, you were wonderful.

LOIS: Nice. Very nice. You're starting to get it.

FRED: You were ... wonderful.

LOIS: Richer. Good work. Now, let it sing! Fill the room. Lois, I saw your performance and you were wonderful.

FRED: Lois, I saw your performance and you were wonderful.

LOIS: Thank you. Would it help if I put my hand on your knee? Call it positive reinforcement.

FRED: That might — *(LOIS places her hand on his thigh.)* Oh yes, you were wonderful. Better than everybody. What an actress. What a performance. God, you were so good. Lois. Lois. Lois.

LOIS: Better, Fred, better. Now, don't lose the edge, because we are ready to go. This is more difficult. ALR. Actress Leaving Restaurant. Hold the mood. Hold it. Gaze at me. Gaze.

FRED: I'm gazing. You were wonderful.

LOIS: You stand first. Good, nice stand. Now, smile at me. *(He smiles.)* Too big. A smaller, gentler "I am in awe of you, and I want people to see me with you" smile. Hold that pose. Nice.

FRED: You were really wonderful. Wonderful. Top notch. Great.

LOIS: Good. Let people realize that I am about to rise and they can get a real long look at me, if they're lucky. OK? Here I come. I'm standing. *(She rises.)*

FRED: I can sense people watching. How long do we stand here? My legs are cramping.

LOIS: Shut up. Gaze at me. Let them wonder, "Is he going home with her? Is he going to spend the night?" OK, deep breath. Now we leave. *(Walking through the audience)* Walk. Slowly. Good. You first, head up, pretend to know someone and nod in their direction. Good. Now, I sweep past you. I walk straight ahead, too important and splendid to acknowledge anyone. *Don't trip!*

FRED: Sorry. Did that spill? So sorry. *(They are outside.)*

LOIS: Good job. I'm proud.

FRED: Thanks.

LOIS: Now comes the really hard part. Since we can't afford a taxi, should we walk home or take the subway? *(They laugh and skip away.)*

LEGAL ACKNOWLEDGMENTS

Copyright Caution

Copyright laws exist to protect the creative and intellectual property rights of creators of original works. All creative works, such as monologues and scripts, are considered copyrighted. There are, however, a number of "fair use" exceptions for educational or instructional purposes related to classroom performance. The monologues and scripts in this volume are fully protected under the copyright laws of the United States, the British Empire, the Dominion of Canada, and all other countries of the Copyright Union. For additional information related to auditions, full-scale productions, or other available scripts, please contact the author or the author's agent at the address listed below.

Chapter 1 An Audition Blueprint

God in Bed by Glenn Alterman. Copyright © 2011 by Glenn Alterman. Reprinted by permission of the author. For additional information please contact the author at 400 West 43rd Street, 7G, New York, New York 10036.

Six Foot Even by Deron Sedy. Copyright © 2007 by Deron Sedy. Reprinted by permission of the author. For additional information please contact the author at deron@digitalderon.com.

Pick Me by Heidi Decker. Copyright © 2012 by Heidi Decker. Reprinted by permission of the author. For additional information please contact the author at heidideckerplays.com.

Whole by Scot Walker. Copyright © 2012 by Scot Walker. Reprinted by permission of the author. For additional information please contact the author at scotwalker2004@yahoo.com.

Pretty for an Asian Girl by Lucy Wang. Copyright © 2013 by Lucy Wang. Reprinted by permission of the author. For additional information please contact the author at anchogirl@yahoo.com or at chickfillet@gmail.com.

My Conversation with Madison. Copyright © 2012 by Amanda Kozik. Reprinted by permission of the author. For additional information please contact the author at Amanda_Kozik@yahoo.com.

Chapter 2 A Time of Innocence

The Darker Face of the Earth by Rita Dove. Copyright © 1998 by Rita Dove. Reprinted by permission of Oberon Books. For additional information please contact the publisher at 521 Caledonian Road, London N7 9RH England.

Out of Sterno by Deborah Zoe Laufer. Copyright © 2009 by Deborah Zoe Laufer. Reprinted by permission of the author's agent. For additional information please contact the author's agent at the William Morris Agency, 1325 Avenue of the Americas, New York, New York 10019.

Stamping, Shouting and Singing Home by Lisa Evans. Copyright © 2004 by Lisa Evans. Reprinted by permission of Oberon Books. For additional information please contact the publisher at 521 Caledonian Road, London N7 9RH England.

The Laramie Project by Moises Kaufman and the Tectonic Theater Project. Copyright © 2000 by Moises Kaufman. Reprinted by permission of the author's agent. For additional information please contact the author's agent at the Creative Artists Agency, 162 Fifth Avenue, 6th Floor, New York, New York 10010.

The Secret Life of Barbie and Mr. Potato Head by Nin Andrews. Copyright © 2010 by Nin Andrews. Reprinted by permission of the author. For additional information please contact the author at 7227 Yellow Creek Drive, Poland, Ohio 44514.

Breathing Corpses by Laura Wade. Copyright © 2008 by Laura Wade. Reprinted by permission of Oberon Books. For additional information please contact the publisher at 521 Caledonian Road, London N7 9RH England.

Some Unfinished Chaos by Evan Guilford Blake. Copyright © 2010 by Evan Guilford Blake. Reprinted by permission of the author. For additional information please contact the author at ejbplaywright@yahoo.com.

A Bird of Prey by Jim Grimsley. Copyright © 1999 by Jim Grimsley. Reprinted by permission of the author's agent. For additional information please contact the author's agent at the Abrams Artists Agency, 275 Seventh Avenue, 26th Floor, New York, New York 10001.

Last Chance Romance by Sam Bobrick. Copyright © 2010 by Sam Bobrick. Reprinted by permission of the author's agent. For additional information please contact the author's agent at the Abrams Artists Agency, 275 Seventh Avenue, 26th Floor, New York, New York 10001.

Slow Falling Bird by Christine Evans. Copyright © 2003 by Christine Evans. Reprinted by permission of the author's agent. For additional information please contact the author's agent at the Peregrine Whittlesey Agency, 279 Central Park West, New York, New York 10024.

Because of Beth by Elana Gartner. Copyright © 2007 by Elana Gartner. Reprinted by permission of the author. For additional information please contact the author at elana@elanagartner.com.

Blue by Ursula Rani Sarma. Copyright © 2002 by Ursula Rani Sarma. Reprinted by permission of Oberon Books. For additional information please contact the publisher at 521 Caledonian Road, London N7 9RH England.

Common Ground by Brendon Votipka. Copyright © 2004 by Brendon Votipka. Reprinted by permission of Playscripts, Inc. For additional information or to purchase acting editions of the script please contact Playscripts, Inc. at http://www.playscripts.com or email info@playscripts.com.

The Columbine Project by Paul Storiale. Copyright © 2009 by Paul Storiale. Reprinted by permission of the author. For additional information please contact the author at pstoriale@gmail.com.

New Age by Vivienne Laxdal. Copyright © 2003 by Vivienne Laxdal. Reprinted by permission of the author. For additional information please contact the author at 90 Rue Cholette, Gatineau, Quebec J8 Y 1J8 Canada.

Baby in the Basement by David-Matthew Barnes. Copyright © 2010 by David-Matthew Barnes. Reprinted by permission of the author. For additional information please contact the author at www.davidmatthewbarnes.com.

Chapter 3 A Time of Rebellion

From *next to normal*. Book and lyrics Copyright © 2010 by Brian Yorkey. Music Copyright © 2010 by Tom Kitt. Published by Theatre Communications Group. Reprinted by permission of Theatre Communications Group. For additional information please contact the publisher at 520 Eighth Avenue, 24th Floor, New York, New York 10018.

Trojan Barbie by Christine Evans. Copyright © 2010 by Christine Evans. Reprinted by permission of the author's agent. For additional information please contact the author's agent at the Peregrine Whittlesey Agency, 279 Central Park West, New York, New York 10024.

Underpants by Wilma Marcus Chandler. Copyright © 2000 by Wilma Marcus Chandler. Reprinted by permission of the author's agent. For additional information please contact the author's agent Marie Winfield, 885 35th Avenue, Santa Cruz, California 95062.

Bunny's Last Night in Limbo by Peter Petralia. Copyright © 2001 by Peter Petralia. Reprinted by permission of the author. For additional information please contact the author at peter@drpetralia.com.

The Arcata Promise by David Mercer. Copyright © 2003 by David Mercer. Reprinted by permission of the author's agent. For additional information please contact the author's agent at Cassarotto Ramsay & Associates, Ltd., Waverley House, 7-12 Noel Street, London W1F 8GQ England.

Third Person: Bonnie and Clyde Redux by Peter Petralia. Copyright © 2010 by Peter Petralia. Reprinted by permission of the author. For additional information please contact the author at peter@drpetralia.com

The Mineola Twins from *The Mammary Plays* by Paula Vogel. Copyright © 1998 by Paula Vogel. Published by Theatre Communications Group. Reprinted by permission of Theatre Communications Group. For additional information please contact the publisher at 520 Eighth Avenue, 24th Floor, New York, New York 10018.

Chapter 4 A Time of Independence

Chapter 5 A Time of Doubt

Tirade by Mary Louise Wilson. Copyright © 2012 by Mary Louise Wilson. Reprinted by permission of the author. For additional information please contact the author at wilson.marylouise@gmail.com.

A Mother's Day Monologue by Glenn Hascall. Copyright © 2004 by Glenn Hascall. Reprinted by permission of the author. For additional information please contact the author at 117 Carefree Lane, Dodge City, Kansas 67801.

Tales from the Tunnel by Troy Diana and James Valletti. Copyright © 2009 by Troy Diana and James Valletti. Reprinted by permission of the authors. For additional information please contact the authors at troydiana1971@yahoo.com or j97elroy@gmail.com.

Don't Breathe on the Job by Allen Davis III. Copyright © 1990 by Allen Davis III. Reprinted by permission of the author. For additional information please contact the author at 484 W. 43rd Street, Apt. 20-F, New York, New York 10036.

I Never Got to Say Good-Bye by Lexanne Leonard. Copyright © 2012 by Lexanne Leonard. Reprinted by permission of the author. For additional information please contact the author at lexleonard2@comcast.net.

Six Views by Lisa Kirazian. Copyright © 2007 by Lisa Kirazian. Reprinted by permission of the author. For additional information please contact the author at kirazian@mac.com.

Chapter 6 A Time of Cynicism

Ruined by Lynn Nottage. Copyright © 2009 by Lynn Nottage. Published by Theatre Communications Group. Reprinted by permission of Theatre Communications Group. For additional information please contact the publisher at 520 Eighth Avenue, 24th Floor, New York, New York 10018.

Night Luster by Laura Harrington. Copyright © 1990 by Laura Harrington. Reprinted by permission of the author's agent. For additional information please contact the author's agent at Bret Adams, Ltd., 448 West 44th Street, New York, New York 10036.

Baggage by Sam Bobrick. Copyright © 2008 by Sam Bobrick. Reprinted by permission of the author's agent. For additional information please contact the author's agent at the Abrams Artists Agency, 275 Seventh Avenue, 26th Floor, New York, New York 10001.

The Pain and the Itch by Bruce Norris. Copyright © 2008 by Bruce Norris. Reprinted by permission of the author's agent. For additional information please contact the author's agent at Harden-Curtis Associates, 214 West 29th Street, Suite 1203, New York, New York 10001.

Stain by Tony Glazer. Copyright © 2009 by Tony Glazer. Reprinted by permission of the author's agent. For additional information please contact the author's agent at Paradigm, 360 Park Avenue South, 16th Floor, New York, New York 10010.

Funny by Christyna Belden. Copyright © 2004 by Christyna Belden. Reprinted by permission of the author. For additional information please contact the author at chibelle@live.com or http://invisible-scars.blogspot.com.

ABOUT THE EDITOR

Gerald Lee Ratliff is the award-winning author of numerous articles, essays, and textbooks in classroom teaching strategies and performance studies. He has served as national president of the Eastern Communication Association; Association of Communication Administration; and Theta Alpha Phi, national theatre honorary fraternity. He has also served on administrative and editorial boards of the American Council of Academic Deans, International Arts Association, National Communication Association, Eastern Communication Association, and the Society of Educators and Scholars.

His publications include popular textbooks in Reader's Theatre, acting styles, musical theatre, dramatic criticism, scene study, oral interpretation of literature, public speaking, and literary case studies of Sophocles' *Oedipus the King* and Machiavelli's *The Prince*. He was awarded the "Distinguished Service Award" by both the Eastern Communication Association and Theta Alpha Phi, named a Fulbright Scholar to China to study non-western drama, selected as a U.S.A. delegate of the John F. Kennedy Center for the Performing Arts to Russia, and has received multiple teaching awards for pioneering innovative curriculum design and pedagogy. He is currently active as a higher education program consultant and workshop facilitator at national academic and professional conferences.

Order Form

Meriwether Publishing Ltd.
PO Box 7710
Colorado Springs, CO 80933-7710
Phone: 800-937-5297 Fax: 719-594-9916
Website: www.meriwether.com

Please send me the following books:

_____	**Audition Monologues for Young Women #2 #BK-B357** edited by Gerald Lee Ratliff *More contemporary auditions for aspiring actresses*	$16.95
_____	**Audition Monologues for Young Women #BK-B323** edited by Gerald Lee Ratliff *Contemporary audition pieces for aspiring actresses*	$16.95
_____	**Young Women's Monologs from Contemporary Plays #BK-B272** edited by Gerald Lee Ratliff *Professional auditions for aspiring actresses*	$15.95
_____	**Young Women's Monologues from Contemporary Plays #2 #BK-B300** edited by Gerald Lee Ratliff *Professional auditions for aspiring actresses*	$15.95
_____	**50/50 Monologues for Student Actors #BK-B321** by Mary Depner *100 monologues for guys and girls*	$15.95
_____	**50/50 Monologues for Student Actors II #BK-B330** by Mary Depner *100 more monologues for guys and girls*	$16.95
_____	**102 Great Monologues #BK-B315** by Rebecca Young *A versatile collection of monologues and duologues for student actors*	$16.95

These and other fine Meriwether Publishing books are available at your local bookstore or direct from the publisher. Prices subject to change without notice. Check our website or call for current prices.

Name: _____ email:_____

Organization name: _____

Address: _____

City: _____ State: _____

Zip: _____ Phone: _____

❑ **Check enclosed**

❑ **Visa / MasterCard / Discover / Am. Express #** _____

Signature: _____ *Expiration date:* _____ / _____ *CVV code:* _____
(required for credit card orders)

Colorado residents: Please add 3% sales tax.
Shipping: Include $3.95 for the first book and 75¢ for each additional book ordered.

❑ *Please send me a copy of your complete catalog of books and plays.*

Order Form

Meriwether Publishing Ltd.
PO Box 7710
Colorado Springs, CO 80933-7710
Phone: 800-937-5297 Fax: 719-594-9916
Website: www.meriwether.com

Please send me the following books:

_____ **Audition Monologues for** $16.95
Young Women #2 #BK-B357
edited by Gerald Lee Ratliff
More contemporary auditions for aspiring actresses

_____ **Audition Monologues for Young Women** $16.95
#BK-B323
edited by Gerald Lee Ratliff
Contemporary audition pieces for aspiring actresses

_____ **Young Women's Monologs from** $15.95
Contemporary Plays #BK-B272
edited by Gerald Lee Ratliff
Professional auditions for aspiring actresses

_____ **Young Women's Monologues from** $15.95
Contemporary Plays #2 #BK-B300
edited by Gerald Lee Ratliff
Professional auditions for aspiring actresses

_____ **50/50 Monologues for Student Actors** $15.95
#BK-B321
by Mary Depner
100 monologues for guys and girls

_____ **50/50 Monologues for Student Actors II** $16.95
#BK-B330
by Mary Depner
100 more monologues for guys and girls

_____ **102 Great Monologues #BK-B315** $16.95
by Rebecca Young
A versatile collection of monologues and duologues for student actors

These and other fine Meriwether Publishing books are available at
your local bookstore or direct from the publisher. Prices subject to
change without notice. Check our website or call for current prices.

Name: _____ email:_____

Organization name: _____

Address: _____

City: _____ State: _____

Zip: _____ Phone: _____

❑ **Check enclosed**

❑ **Visa / MasterCard / Discover / Am. Express #** _____

| | *Expiration* | | *CVV* |
Signature: _____ *date:* _____ / _____ *code:* _____
(required for credit card orders)

Colorado residents: Please add 3% sales tax.
Shipping: Include $3.95 for the first book and 75¢ for each additional book ordered.

❑ *Please send me a copy of your complete catalog of books and plays.*